eating pizza
backwards,
and other adventures

eating pizza backwards,
and other adventures

a mom, a daughter,
a life unexpected

Eileen Flood O'Connor

PALMETTO
PUBLISHING
Charleston, SC
www.PalmettoPublishing.com

Copyright © 2026 by Eileen Flood O'Connor

All rights reserved

No portion of this book may be reproduced, stored in a retrieval system, or transmitted in any form by any means—electronic, mechanical, photocopy, recording, or other—except for brief quotations in printed reviews, without prior permission of the author.

Paperback ISBN: 9798822981805
eBook ISBN: 9798822981812

for Will, Patrick and Jay

Contents

Foreword vii

A Letter to Myself on Diagnosis Day 1

Eating Pizza Backwards. 9

Groundhog Day. 15

Look to the Strangers 21

A Pocket Full of Joy 27

A Dog Named Pablo 35

I am a mom. I am that mom. 43

A Tale of Two Moms 49

Ode to the Virtual Circle of Special Needs Moms 57

Road Trip 63

Surviving a Special Needs Marriage. 69

Seizures and Silver Linings 77

Relying on Science, Going on Faith 85

Finding Awe in the Every Day 91

Finding Joy in Aisle Nine 97

Thirteen 103

Losing Pop-Pop	111
A Time to Grow	117
Point to Happy	123
On Losing a Good Dog	129
Lessons on Winning and Living	137
Magical Thinking	143
Celebrating the Small Things this Christmas	149
Cookie Monster	157
The Helpers	165
Happiness is a Bunch of Bananas	173
Author's Note	179
Acknowledgements	181
About the Author, Eileen Flood O'Connor	191
About the Cover Artist, Patrick Ford O'Connor	191

Foreword

Before most of us become parents, we have a vision of our future family, maybe a certain number of children, healthy, bright and curious. Some might dream of athletic ability or musical talent. Others might imagine a tech savvy kid who will create the next big invention. And all, I venture to guess, celebrate the gift of the well-rounded child whose life is free of travail, who is everyone's friend, generous of heart and spirit.

And yet, the world has a way of showing us how little we control the script. Dreams motivate and connect us as human beings, but it's the way we respond to reality, it's finding resilience when real life unfolds, that can make the difference in your perspective. Two decades ago, when our family was going through a particularly hard time, a friend said something I think of often. "In life, you play the hand you're dealt, but the trick is to never stop trying to get your hands on the deck."

The essays in this book are a reminder that we all have the ability to write our story, to emphasize the positive and the possible, to choose the lens through which we see the world. It's about looking for the blessings, not counting the curveballs; finding joy in everyday moments and life's inevitable plot twists.

EATING PIZZA BACKWARDS, AND OTHER ADVENTURES

As a parent, most of us would do anything for our children; take any pain upon ourselves to make it better for them. This was my very first thought, in 2000, when one of our twins was diagnosed as deaf due to a genetic abnormality my husband and I hadn't known anything about. I can still remember the interior of the office I was in when the doctor made his matter-of-fact pronouncement. I can recall, bizarrely, that his socks had a roaring tiger on them, the image so incongruous with what he was telling me: that my daughter's world would be constricted and forever altered by the loss of sound. Whether he meant to or not, the doctor began to smother any tendril of hope I desperately needed, as I tried to absorb the shock of the diagnosis. He was already minimizing my daughter's life, snuffing out joy and limiting possibility before we'd left the building.

I went home and cried. Would she play and attend school alongside her sister? Would she talk with friends on a telephone or hear her own baby cry? After I got my tears out though, I understood that I had work to do. I had the power to create a world in which Nora could have choices, opportunities for language and learning, hearing aids at her early stage to bathe her in spoken words during those critical first years of brain development. My goal was to do all I could to help her live and thrive in a world that would see her as disabled. All I could do was my very best. That would have to be enough. My job as a parent was to help Nora walk through the

FOREWORD

world with all her gifts, and to be seen, not as someone with a disability, but a person with a *different ability*.

Eileen O'Connor's beautiful collection of essays is like a necklace, where each strung pearl is a taut little nugget of wisdom, an insight into the many ways her daughter, Erin, has taught their family magical lessons about living and being in the moment. Erin was born "on the spectrum," and in those early days after diagnosis, Eileen's first essay is an unforgettable letter to herself, acknowledging the shock of receiving an unexpected diagnosis and life path yet ultimately telling herself she could do hard things as she steps into battle mode for her little girl.

Raising children with or without disabilities is challenging in today's world, and the stories in this book are universal, depicting the myriad heartbreaks, triumphs, joy and sorrow that all parents experience at different times and in different measures. These essays are a reminder that light and beauty lurk even in the difficult moments, and that the gift of the different ability is to look at the world with new eyes, to embrace a novel approach to eating pizza, to delight in dancing trees, to relish the reassuring love and kisses of a drooling Labrador - and to experience gratitude at every turn. That's the gift that Erin and her mom have given to the rest of us, and we are richer for it.

Lee Woodruff
Author

"To survive you must tell stories."

Umberto Eco

A Letter to Myself on Diagnosis Day

Ok – Breathe.

Yes, you heard right. Erin was diagnosed with something called Duplication 15 Syndrome. I know. What the heck? That wasn't in the realm of things we worried about. She has ten fingers and ten toes, but she also has an extra part of Chromosome 15.

Yes, you heard right – developmental delays, speech, language, motor impairments, autism. No this is not good – but it confirms what you've been thinking for the past 22 months. Something was not right. So, in a way that's a positive? Your instincts were right.

But I know you're not up for feeling very positive right now. And that's ok. It's ok to take some time to be sad – and to process what the very curt geneticist outlined. But don't ignore it because you're mad at him. Don't space out and slip into denial.

You heard him mention PT, OT, Speech Therapy, Early Intervention. Get on that.

And do not dismiss that scary sounding therapy: Applied Behavior Analysis — just because the slide show at the seminar made it look cruel and unusual. And do not ignore the urging of the woman from the agency who suggests a home-based 40 hour a week ABA program just because you don't like the way she sits on your sofa and sizes up your mess. Do not dismiss her because you suspect she just wants to get Erin out of the classroom.

It's ok. Let your guard down long enough to realize that oddly enough there are people out there who want to help Erin — and know how. Poor bedside manner aside, this woman knows what she's talking about. ABA will help. It's not going to isolate her. Erin needs it more than she needs to sit alone in the corner of a classroom spinning the wheels of a Tonka Truck. It will help her. It will draw her out of herself. She will learn to sit and to listen and to respond. She will learn to communicate.

Steel yourself. It will not be easy — it will be gut wrenching to hear your three-year-old wailing because she doesn't have the words to say that she just wants to sit on the floor and admire the ceiling fan. You don't want her to go through

A LETTER TO MYSELF ON DIAGNOSIS DAY

life comfortable and happy only when she gets what she wants. And you do not want her to want that. ABA will take her a long way.

But when you feel she has plateaued and you learn of new therapies, don't torture yourself about leaving her team of teachers. They know how you feel – you can never thank them enough. But it's time. It will be ok. Be confident. You are the mom. And you are a good mom.

Give yourself a break. Don't feel guilty. Don't blame yourself and don't blame your husband. Don't blame the move to London or that you sometimes drank unfiltered tap water – or a glass of wine.

Don't blame the cups of coffee.

Don't blame EU emissions standards.

Do not blame Tony Blair.

Bad things happen for no reason all the time. You know this. Don't feel guilty. You did what you were supposed to. You took the vitamins. You avoided soft cheese. No, you didn't deserve this, but people don't get what they deserve. They get what they get. "You get what you get, and you don't get upset." In a few years your son will skip home from preschool reciting this mantra.

He will still get upset when he doesn't get what he wants. And you can too – for a short time. Then get on with it and realize that while this diagnosis is bad – it is not the end of the world. In fact, it will bring many beautiful things.

This diagnosis will bruise but not break your heart, your family, your marriage. It will strengthen and enrich every relationship in your life. It will stretch your soul. But before you can begin to understand this you have a lot of work to do – and so many exceptionally kind people to help you along the way.

Some you have known all along, some you will know for only moments – but in a smile or a word they will remind you that you can do this. You can't see them from here, from this awful chair, in this awful office, on this awful day – but they are out there waiting for you.

So, get going and enjoy your daughter. Don't focus on what she can't do or is not doing by the time she is "supposed" to be doing it. Celebrate what she manages to do on her very own timetable.

Know that she will learn to walk and talk. In fact, one day, she will walk miles beside a dog named Pablo and sing about the sun and trees and how they dance in the wind.

A LETTER TO MYSELF ON DIAGNOSIS DAY

She will learn to hug and to love. Hug and love her back and go home and hold your son.

Hug him as much as you can and celebrate his milestones too. Don't be sad when he surpasses Erin. Incredibly enough you will have two more boys who will do the same.

This is ok. You will be blessed with four very different children with unique personalities, interests, and strengths. Don't compare and contrast. Celebrate them. Listen to them. Learn from them.

This will not be an easy road – your sadness will be cyclical – but on the darkest days know that it will always abate and the good and beautiful moments and people will far outnumber the bad. Have faith in this. Have faith in faith – and know that Erin will one day teach you and all who cross her path what matters most: love and hugs – and dancing trees.

Get going…

"People who have not been to Narnia sometimes think that a thing cannot be good and terrible at the same time."

C.S. Lewis
The Chronicles of Narnia

*

"Love begins at home."

Mother Teresa

Eating Pizza Backwards

I recently came across a publication for people whose lives have been touched by a wide range of disabilities. It was inspiring to read one uplifting story after another about how this or that diagnosis had turned out to be a "gift" – and how the writer wouldn't change a thing about the person they love, or their own condition. I often share my own stories about my daughter and the perspective she gives and the exceptional people who have come into our lives because of her disability.

Many on the milder side of the autism spectrum embrace their diagnosis, reject the term "disability" and instead celebrate the uniqueness autism has bestowed on them. If given the choice, Temple Grandin, autism's unofficial spokesperson has said: "If I could snap my fingers and become non-autistic, I would not." She asserts and rightly so that she is: "Different, not less."

As the autism community prepares to kick off Autism Awareness Month with a celebration of World Autism

Day on April 2nd, I wonder if by embracing and spotlighting the many positive sides of different, we are somehow rounding off the edges of this complex neurological disorder in a way that makes it difficult for some to say this is in fact not so fabulous. I'm familiar with a few who feel this way.

If my sons could snap their fingers and change their older sister's disability, they would in a heartbeat. They ask me all the time if there will ever be a cure for autism.

Last fall a close friend received a cancer diagnosis. It was thankfully caught early and after aggressive treatment, she's now cancer free. My sons were quick to ask if we could do something like that for Erin.

They love their sister, but they don't love that she has autism.

It's not funny for them when she has a meltdown in a public place. They don't like that she can't dress or care for herself. That she screams through a shower. That she often gets into their stuff and scribbles on their books or tears up a poster or important school form. That she reads to herself loudly regardless of whether they're watching a movie or a game and the score is tied with ten seconds left. That she takes up so much of Mom's time, attention, thoughts and concern.

"You love Erin the most." I've heard this more than once – particularly when a demand has been placed on them and not her.

They get embarrassed and frustrated and scared about what the future holds for her and them. Where will she live? Who will care for her? Will she go to college? Will she get married?

When my oldest son was in kindergarten and had a friend over for the first time, he prepped the playmate with a long list of potential pitfalls: "I just want to tell you that my sister has autism and she might jump up and down in front of the TV or spill her juice or pinch you. Oh, and she eats her pizza backwards!" (The friend, undeterred by all red flags, entered the house and an exceedingly uneventful playdate ensued.)

Insecurities aside, I like to think it's their love for their sister that makes them hate her diagnosis. They would like to see her live a typical life – or rather, a life just like theirs. She should be running off to practice and studying for the next big test. Helping them navigate social media. Sharing inside jokes. Watching movies with them, as opposed to Barney reruns.

I know if Erin were "typical" there's no guarantee they'd share a rosy relationship and life would be all milk and honey. There would be other hurdles and issues. I'm sure there are still plenty ahead.

I'm also aware that some people with autism or who have children with autism feel that they have been blessed and given a window into a special world – a world they would never have known if they had not been born with their disability. There's no denying that.

And while this is true to an extent in our home – yes, Erin has taught us to smile at the often overlooked and unexpected, to hug and to love unconditionally – if her brothers could alter the conditions of her life – remove the impediments – I know they would.

As much as I want them to accept and to embrace what life gives, I don't want them to feel guilty for wishing that Erin could tie her shoes or write her name or talk to them about how life or Mom can be so mean and unfair and even fun sometimes.

I want them to know it's ok to love their sister, while not loving that she has autism.

> "We shall not cease from exploration
> And at the end of all our exploring
> Will be to arrive where we started
> And to know the place for the first time"
>
> T.S. Elliot
> *"Little Gidding"*

Groundhog Day

Most days we manage to stay on task and in the moment. We get up, brush our teeth, find or don't find our shoes and clothes and favorite hat. We catch the bus and the carpool, go our separate ways for a few hours, and then regroup for the afternoon's festivities of snacks, sports, homework, dinner, showers (maybe), sleep and the dream of doing it all over again.

It's our very own version of the movie, *Groundhog Day*, in which Bill Murray maddeningly gets stuck repeating the same day over and over again. But for our family of four kids and a dog, as long as we stick to the schedule and no one gets hurt, I have come to realize Groundhog Day has its perks.

Any parenting expert, almost any parent, will report that kids thrive on a predictable routine. Parents of children with autism know that some kids take "routine" to a whole other level. In our kitchen we have a dry-erase board and every night at Erin's prompting I write the schedule for the next day.

She smiles and claps in delight as I record what time the bus will arrive, what time it will deliver her home, what classes or activities lay in store, will there be visitors or guests, will there be a trip to the library, CVS or the grocery store? For Erin a foreseeable routine brings comfort and joy – and there is magic in the mundane.

I'm not a planner by nature. In my former life there was nothing I relished more than a day that held nothing but possibility. Erin, and her younger brothers to a lesser extent, have conditioned me to understand and to embrace the merits of routine – and have taught me how tricky life can be when we veer off course.

While other kids celebrate a snow or vacation day, Erin grows anxious. Now, I do too. I frantically scribble a list of minutiae: wake up, feed the dog, eat breakfast, brush our teeth, watch a show, read a book, go for a walk, bake cookies. I insert a lot of smiley faces throughout to reassure that this uncharted terrain is ok, it is manageable, and we will get through. But there are unavoidable days and moments that defy routine and my smiley faces.

On one recent night, the boys brought up "the future." In most families, I imagine, this is a reasonable topic. Kids everywhere like to ponder: Where will I live? Who will I

GROUNDHOG DAY

be? But in our home, this line of hypothetical questioning leads to shaky ground.

While we're all ok with the fact that Jay, the youngest, may never play in the NBA, we are less ok with the unlikely prospect of Erin ever living independently. With the boys I feel confident in my hopes that they will one day find a job and friends and live on their own or with someone who loves them.

Erin, I don't know, and I have no real answer to her brothers' questions: "Who will she live with? Who will take care of her? Will they be nice to her?"

"She will be safe and happy and cared for," I tell them. But I don't know if this is true.

What I do know is what Erin asks me to see and to celebrate every day: the sun comes up, the sun goes down and in between we have a day.

We have our routine.

We have our dry-erase board. Its' confines keep us in check, contained and content.

Thankfully there is space for only so much: four kids, one dog, one mom, one day. Repeat.

"I have always depended on the kindness of strangers."

Tony Kushner
Angels in America

Look to the Strangers

I dropped Erin off late to school today. Her aide, Lisa, met us at the main office and Erin immediately enveloped her in one of her signature bear hugs. Lisa hugged her back and told Erin their class was in the library knowing that would make Erin smile. It did. As I watched them walk away hand in hand down the hallway, I paused to take a picture. It was a moment I wanted to keep and to carry around all day.

Driving home I thought of a friend who recently shared that when her daughters were younger and they were upset about something bad that had happened in their town or some event they heard of in the news, she would borrow a lesson from Fred Rogers and remind them that though frightening things happen, it's important to look for the helpers. You will always find people who are helping.

As a parent whose child received a life altering diagnosis, the unexpected and the scary has happened and I am always on the lookout for the helpers. I cannot get

Erin through her day without them. I need someone to walk her down the hallway and to her classroom safely. And when that someone takes the time to hold her hand and to make her smile, my gratitude knows no bounds.

This leave taking – the act of entrusting your child to the care of another is a rite of passage for all parents, but for those with children who cannot communicate the details of their days, it is a leap of immeasurable faith.

If I could describe what it means to be a special needs parent in one word, it would be appreciative. You appreciate the smallest things your child says or does – but you also appreciate beyond measure the people who come into your life to help.

Over the course of Erin's thirteen years, I've relied on a wide safety net of family, friends, doctors, teachers, aides, as well as a long trail of anonymous men and women whose smile or passing kindness have softened our often rough and sometimes scary days.

When Erin was seven-years-old, I lost her while shopping with my sister at a clothing store on Manhattan's Upper West Side. We each thought the other had Erin. When I realized this was not the case, my heart stopped.

I anticipated the sound of a car crash, imagining she had wandered out of the store and on to Broadway.

As employees blocked the exits and conducted a frantic search, a woman appeared at the store front asking if anyone had lost a little girl. The woman and her three friends had found Erin hesitating at the top of an escalator in a nearby store. Erin, who is captivated by the movement of escalators but has trouble timing her step to board, was found at the base of the store's escalator clutching a bright, green t-shirt with an image of *Curious George* emblazoned across the front. A *GAP* price tag dangled from one of the sleeves.

Finding Erin encircled by this group of women, I think I said thank you, though I may have said nothing. They seemed to think nothing of it. "Good timing, glad we could help," and they moved on their way.

It took me weeks to recover.

I still get weak thinking about it – both the feeling of losing her – and the appreciation I felt for these complete strangers – helpers who found my daughter and took the time to find me.

They are everywhere.

Sometimes we know their name. And sometimes they float in and out of your day, your life, so briefly, you barely get a chance to acknowledge them, let alone stop and take a picture. Either way I carry them with me forever.

"That is part of the beauty of all literature. You discover that your longings are universal longings, that you're not lonely and isolated from anyone. You belong."

F. Scott Fitzgerald

*

"Sometimes the dustiest cover hides the best book. Sometimes the best cup is chipped."

Belle
Beauty and the Beast

A Pocket Full of Joy

Books, bookstores, and libraries often feel like an endangered species. As more people spend their lives online, the need for a physical space to house and browse bookshelves has been called into question. However, there remains a segment of the population for whom this online nether world does not translate, and for whom "logging on" will never compare to "walking in" to a building filled not only with books – but with people who love them. My daughter is one of them.

Unlike many girls her age, Erin does not have a phone, an email address, Instagram or Snapchat. To communicate with her, you pretty much have to be standing right in front of her and even then demand that she look you in the eye – a request which may or may not be followed depending on her mood and the person making the ask.

There are a magical few, however, who readily command her attention and sustain her eye contact. For several years now the staff at our local library have not only welcomed Erin – and her service dog, a Black Lab named Pablo – but also engaged her in a continuous conversation.

Erin has always loved books: the way they look and feel, the pictures, the pages, the words. She is drawn to their physicality – generally the bigger and heavier the better. They are her constant companions – she is never without a book or three tucked under her arm or into bed beside her.

While language came late and communication still poses its challenges, Erin, ironically, feels most at home in a space which reveres and celebrates words. She taught herself to read by memorizing what words look like. She learned that words together combine to tell a story and it is in these stories that she has found a medium that explains and enhances her experience of the world – and the passage of time itself.

Erin marks the calendar year through books: books about reindeer and snowmen, hearts and Valentines, Shamrocks and Spring, books about Easter eggs and the Fourth of July, sandcastles and fireflies, books about back-to-school and falling leaves, apple and pumpkin picking, Jack-O-Lanterns, turkeys and giving thanks. She experiences and expresses unparalleled joy upon discovering Christmas books again.

To her delight and amazement, at the library Erin has found a group of kindred spirits who gauge and celebrate the season in much the same way. She marvels at the topical display of shiny hard covered books as she enters the children's reading room. She, and I, appreciate beyond measure that in this sacred space she has found a few individuals who are not only as assiduous about categorizing, locating and loving books as she, but are so very patient and kind.

Erin is not the most silent of library visitors. As she bounces up and down the aisles happily greeting all who cross her path be they preschoolers or Peter Rabbit and I implore her to keep her voice down, the librarians say nothing but: "What can I help you find?"

On a recent visit Erin asked the librarian if she could locate "the nursery book about the pie." Before I could offer a few more specifics, the woman immediately turned to her computer, typed a few words and began to sing: "Ahh, yes, Erin, sing a song of sixpence a pocket full of rye, four and twenty blackbirds … I know that one…let's see

– and here it is…" And without saying another word the two of them disappeared behind a bookcase only to return moments later with the book – which indeed had a picture of a pie and a smattering of blackbirds on its cover.

On our next visit it was a "blue dictionary" she was after. Undoubtedly, she had spied one in her classroom or school library, which she was not allowed to take home. Upon announcing that she would like a "blue dictionary," the librarian did not roll her eyes or tell her that sounded like a stretch as I might in an impatient moment, but instead replied: "Hmmm, let's take a look over here," and led her and Pablo off to the resource room from which she returned clutching a sizeable dictionary – emblazoned with a spine of royal blue.

The library is a place where one must interact if only with a few words and engage with the world and those in it. For Erin it offers an invaluable exercise in communication. In the beginning the tangible exchange of a book from one hand to another was very hard for her because she does not like to let go of her books, even for the time it takes them to be scanned. Yet over time she learned to wait and to trust that the librarian would give her back the book. And as her familiarity with this space has grown, so has her language. Every trip provides a unique opportunity to practice how to say "Hello," and to ask "How are you? Have you seen *The Big Red Barn*" and "Yes, it is a wonderful book and thank you for finding it for me." "Good-bye library – see you next time."

"A dog has no use for fancy cars, big homes, or designer clothes. A waterlogged stick will do just fine. A dog doesn't care if you're rich or poor, educated, or illiterate, clever or dull. Give him your heart and he will give you his. How many people can you say that about? How many people can make you feel rare and pure and special? How many people can make you feel extraordinary?"

John Grogan
Marley and Me

A Dog Named Pablo

As parents we encourage our children to just be themselves. Time after time I impart this advice to my sons whenever they express anxiety about a new social situation. However, over the years I have hesitated to give Erin the same advice.

Though my husband and I and a rare few will always delight in Erin's uniqueness, we know the world is not often quite as accepting. Since her earliest days we, along with a host of specialists, have imposed a rigorous regime and barked a litany of instructions to help her function within the parameters of what social norms demand.

"Quiet voice. Calm body. Personal space. Look her in the eye. Say hello. Say goodbye. Say thank you." It's hard enough to assimilate and make friends as a typical kid, for children on the spectrum their quirks, language, physical and behavioral challenges can make it next to impossible.

When Erin was nine-years-old we welcomed someone into our family who, for the first time in her life, demanded nothing from her – a friend who was not bothered by her tendency to jump up and down and flap her hands, who did not mind her difficulties with voice modulation and spatial relations – who in fact welcomed and encouraged her need for close proximity. This person genuinely loved and accepted her for who she is – for being herself – and showered her with a level of affection, devotion and patience that is beyond human – largely because he is just that.

He is a dog. A very special dog named Pablo,

Erin calls Pablo, a Black Lab with big brown eyes, her "best buddy." Sometimes, to her brothers' infinite amusement, she refers to him as Smee, because he often wears a red bandana like the deckhand in *Peter Pan*.

Pablo came to us through a program that trains dogs to work with children with autism and their families. The primary goal of this program is to provide safety and specifically to prevent them from bolting or wandering in public. While this added security provides tremendous relief for parents who may have dreaded and avoided public outings with their children, the gifts that the children and families receive from this program are manifold.

One of Erin's favorite activities is walking to town with Pablo. She does not participate in organized sports, so this serves as her central means of exercise. With Pablo at her side, they log several miles a week, his steady gait keeping her grounded and focused on the road ahead. He also helps her to engage and connect with all who cross their path. They have become a familiar sight along the route. Neighbors, kids, and adults alike wave from cars and greet them along the way.

Though Erin is the main recipient of Pablo's attention and affection, our entire family has gained immeasurably from his presence in our life. Behind every child diagnosed with autism is a family affected and forever changed. While Erin's younger brothers have never known a life other than one in which their older sister behaves differently than their friends' siblings, I know there are days they wish for her and for themselves a different experience.

Every time we enter a new situation or setting, anxiety levels rise. We can never be certain how Erin will react. Will something set her off? Will we have to leave immediately? Will Bill or I leave with her? Who will stay with the boys? Or will we all just exit and call it a day? There's a fair amount of uncertainty regarding even the most mundane outings.

While a dog does not change the fact that their sister has autism, he certainly has enhanced the equation. Pablo has plowed through many a social barrier not only for Erin but for her brothers as well. When approached by this gentle giant sporting his bright blue service dog vest, people naturally let down their guard. Pablo puts people at ease and allows Erin to interact and communicate in a way that seems natural – almost typical.

People of all ages stop to ask if they can pet her dog. They ask his name and age and how long we've had him. Suddenly the conversation is set in motion and smiles are exchanged as Pablo happily steps into the spotlight and the rest of us find ourselves experiencing a rare moment of calm within the confines of a public space.

Pablo has not negated the challenges Erin or our family face, but he has helped to bring about a fair amount of love and healing. He is less a dog and more a 90-pound shedding, drooling, best friend who wants no one to change, who loves without conditions, who stands resolutely by your side as you have a complete meltdown because you can't find the purple one. Someone who kisses tears and wayward crumbs off your face and will play fetch when everyone else has gone inside. Someone who will jump on your bed and keep you company as you sleep, who will listen to you read for hours and not correct a word, who does not care if your socks match or your shoes for that matter. A companion who will walk for miles by your side and sit for hours as you search for just the right library book, who will never say it's time to go, we are late, you're taking too long, stop acting that way – someone who just wants you to be yourself and stay close and when mom's not looking to share your hamburger.

Many ask what exactly Pablo does for Erin. There are so many answers – and then there is only one. He loves her.

> "Perhaps it takes courage to raise children."
>
> John Steinbeck
> *East of Eden*

In May 2016 a 400-pound gorilla named Harambe was shot and killed at the Cincinnati Zoo after a 4-year-old climbed into its enclosure. Many fiercely criticized the mother for losing track of her son.

I am a mom.
I am that mom.

I have four kids just a few years apart. I have managed to lose each of them at different times for varying amounts of time.

When we lived in New York City, my son, a ball of pent-up energy, would race ahead of me on his scooter while I ran to catch up, pushing his sister in her stroller, screaming for him to slow down, to wait for me, to stay within, if not my reach, at least my sight.

I'd hold my breath when he turned the corner for his preschool and the few minutes I could not seem him. Should he have been abducted in the time it took me to reach him, it would have been my fault.

Erin, like many kids with autism, has always tended to wander. She is distracted and fascinated by escalators, books, and animals. She would have wanted to touch and hug a live gorilla.

I have lost her in the city. I have lost her in the country. I have lost her in my own home. It was never my intention to lose her. I lost my mind every time I did.

During a family gathering at our home when I thought she was upstairs reading, a friend found her sitting in the middle of the road in front of our house. Had something happened to her in any of those locations, it would have been my fault.

The level of venom and vitriol unleashed at this woman, this mom, blows my mind. I wonder if her critics realize she did not arrive at the zoo that morning, a bevy of kids in tow with the intent to lose a child or to set in motion the demise of a majestic animal. I wonder if her critics have ever tried to corral a group of young children. I wonder if they know that often they move in opposite directions or simultaneously drop their ice cream and need their shoes tied. I wonder if they know that sometimes kids don't listen, sometimes they whine and cry and fight and distract you from yourself.

I AM A MOM. I AM THAT MOM.

I wonder if they know that sometimes they shake loose and run away further than you can see. I wonder if they know the terror that strikes a mom when they are out of her sight.

I wonder if her critics have ever loved someone who cannot care for themselves – someone whose safety and life depends on you. I wonder if they know what it feels like to lose someone you love. And I wonder what they would sanction to get that person back.

"If you become a bird and fly away from me," said his mother,
"I will be a tree that you come home to..."

Margaret Wise Brown
The Runaway Bunny

A Tale of Two Moms

Having wrestled the boys to bed, I return to the kitchen to find Vangie reading Erin the Disney story, *Lilo and Stitch*. I begin to load the dishwasher as Vangie's soft voice floats over the kitchen island.

"Ohana means family." Lilo said. "Family means nobody gets left behind."

I glance at my daughter cuddled beside Vangie, who has helped us care for Erin and her three younger brothers for the past four years. This lifesaver of a woman has a 15-year-old daughter in the Philippines whom she has not seen in 10 years. Vangie came here to work and regularly sends money back to her parents and siblings who care for her daughter.

I wonder if Lilo's words strike her as they do me. If they do, there is no visible hesitation, and she does not miss a beat in the story. She well knows that it is best to keep a steady pace with Erin who studies Vangie's lips — entranced as much by the consistent production of words as the story itself.

Erin is drawn to repetition in a variety of forms and is captivated by predictable progressions: the recitation of words, the tapping of fingers, the rotation of ceiling fans. I have come to accept, somewhat, that Erin is as thrilled by the telling as the tale itself. Erin has always loved books – being read to, as well as flipping through the pages, studying the text, pouring over the illustrations. In a book the words keep coming and the pages keep turning. It's all very predictable and reassuring. However, not all stories are as predictable as the mechanisms through which they are told. And neither Vangie nor I know how the stories of our daughters will end.

Desperate to become a U.S. citizen so that her daughter can live with her here, Vangie applied for a green card years ago. Since then, she met an American, originally from her country, to whom she is now engaged. As she prepares her application for citizenship through marriage, she can simultaneously submit a petition to have her daughter come live with her. However, she only has until her daughter turns 18, when she will no longer be classified a minor and deemed too old to enter the country as her mother's daughter.

A TALE OF TWO MOMS

Vangie talks with her daughter weekly. She knows her progress in school, how she gets on with her peers, schoolgirl crushes and social outings. She charts her growth through photos, noting new hairstyles, dresses, how much she has come to resemble her own mother. She has celebrated birthdays, graduations, family milestones – all at a distance. It's impossible to say how much she has missed while striving to give her daughter something better. Because in the end, Vangie's daughter is a world away.

Sometimes I can't help but feel this way about Erin too. Though she has been right here beside me all along, I have spent much of her childhood distracted, trying to figure out a way to reach her. Over the years I have enlisted a small army of specialists to help us "breakthrough" to teach her how to walk, to talk, to play and to interact in some sort of meaningful way with her family and the world around her. I've read the books, attended the seminars, implemented the diets and explored the alternative therapies.

The theory goes that if left to their own devices, children on the spectrum might fold in on themselves, so tantalized by their own experience of the world they may be unable or unwilling to look beyond themselves. Without the right therapy, they will lack the tools to ever purposefully interact with others. Whatever their cognitive abilities, they must be consistently pried from their comfort zone, whether their fascination be lining up match box cars, discussing the solar system or studying sunlight as it falls through a windowpane.

When Erin was 18-months-old, before we knew but had an inkling that something was not right we brought her to a neurologist who after a brief exam hastily scribbled down the number for Early Intervention and directed us to call immediately: "With these kids you have a window and if you don't act now you could lose her." His words terrified me. Erin sat bouncing on my lap happily paging through a picture book, which at the time seemed so typical – how could I "lose her?"

The years since have been a constant struggle to avoid finding the answer.

Some days Erin is more with us than others. We do all we can to keep her engaged, to keep the dialogue and connections going. As our family grew, we hired Vangie to help us keep Erin's downtime to a minimum and to keep her from retreating into her own world. When I become frustrated with the unpredictable nature of Erin's days

A TALE OF TWO MOMS

and nights, Vangie's endless patience and calm amazes and inspires me. But as I have learned, she has more experience with a life of waiting to connect with a child and living with the uncertainty and hope that it will ever happen at all.

In Vangie's book there are no hard and fast answers or definitions of family or love or how one relates to the other. It's an unpredictable story with an unforeseeable end. As mothers we do the due diligence, we file the petitions, submit the paperwork, enlist the experts – we do what they say we must do to get our children back, but still we are left to wonder will we really ever find them – will we reach them – in time.

"I'll find it! Cried Horton. I'll find it or burst!
I SHALL find my friends on my small
speck of dust!"

Dr. Seuss
Horton Hears a Who

Ode to the Virtual Circle of Special Needs Moms

It's official: a *New York Times*' Op-Ed reports: "Scholars have analyzed the data and social media is making us miserable." I don't think this is breaking news for anyone.

As the mother of a special needs child, I don't find this much of a revelation. Everyone is doing something more exciting and fabulous than my daughter. We are still working on independent living skills, so a good day is getting our socks on - generally, not documented.

Our reality vs most social media posts does not make me particularly sad – or miserable. It's just the way it is. In fact, while I understand the gist – I don't find the report completely accurate.

Through social media I've been fortunate to correspond with a small and powerful army of moms whose children share Erin's diagnosis. These moms are as indelible as the chromosomal anomaly that brings them together. In the safe haven of a 'closed' online world, these women create a safety net for each other.

They are strong, but they are struggling. Many feel that they are failing. But for every mom who says: "Help. I'm scared. I'm confused. I'm not sure how much more I can take," there are ten who respond: "Me too. Hang in there. This worked for us. This is really hard."

If it takes a village to raise a child, it takes several to raise one with special needs. I have been lucky to find friends and professionals who provide consistent support. We are fortunate to have an understanding, extended family and network of friends.

But the reality that hits in the form of a three am seizure, a new, aggressive behavior and a very uncertain future can isolate and overwhelm. There is an immeasurable sense of relief and camaraderie in knowing someone else is walking the same road – wherever that road may be.

Through social media I have found a virtual foxhole of moms, reporting live from the trenches. We take meticulous notes and learn from each other's perspectives. Together we endure and provide cover from challenging school personnel, ill-suited medications, 'off' days and misguided strangers.

ODE TO THE VIRTUAL CIRCLE OF SPECIAL NEEDS MOMS

And yes, if I had only 'typical' Instagram, Face Book posts and Twitter feeds, not to mention the barrage of sports and academic accolades reported in our local paper and school pick up lines to bounce my experience off, I would probably feel alone and possibly less than. I understand why and how, if not approached judiciously, social media can make voyeurs miserable. I consistently remind myself and my teenage sons of the façade.

In light of all that is fantastical out there, I am thankful to my online mom village for telling it like it is – and how they wish it could be. I appreciate their detailing the small victories, the comical moments and soul crushing days – because they are mine. I salute and am inspired by the intense commitment these women show their children and each other. Time after time, from across the globe, they are there for each other.

Some have partners, resources support systems in place. Many do not. The divorce rate is high among the special needs community.

Parenting a child with a debilitating condition is intense and ripe for strife. Behaviors, sleep deprivation, the unmanageability of it all overwhelms. So many marriages fall apart.

Things fall apart, but these special moms hold it together by reaching out, asking for help and propping each other up. They read and research, they lose sleep and sanity, but they refuse to lose their kids – and they refuse to leave any mom behind.

I am humbled by and grateful for these moms, their grit, their strength, their love – and the platform that brings us together.

"Getting there is half the fun, come share it with me."

Kermit the Frog

Road Trip

It's raining in South Georgia. Traffic is backed up for miles. Anxiety mounts as I check to see if our sole passenger is still napping in the back. When traveling with Erin moments of peace like this are gold dust - on a 1200-mile journey you hate to squander them standing still.

I'm at the wheel which I stole from Bill at the last pit stop, slipping into the driver's seat as he waited for a *Happy Meal*. An earlier music search made Erin stir so we've settled on silence as we study the pine trees that line I-95.

Every now and then as the traffic eases and I speed up Bill raises his hands dramatically as if bracing for a crash. Given the requisite silence I can't respond as I'd like. Instead, I suggest he close his eyes.

He pretends to relax but he's not comfortable with this arrangement. After 22 years we have our roles and routine. He drives. I play copilot, DJ, sharer of fun facts from random reading material and purveyor of snacks. For a long time this worked out fine.

Early in our marriage we lived in London and spent many weekends exploring the countryside. British accents, idioms and earnest-sounding weathermen were a novelty. We couldn't get enough of the BBC's news, interviews, game shows – and the newly released album, *Babylon*, by David Gray.

We spent half our time meandering down uncharted paths, slowing down for sheep crossing and the occasional tractor. I'd sprawl colorful maps across the dash reciting the names and history of tiny towns, ancient ruins and rolling terrain from travel guides all the while reminding him to keep to the right side of the road.

"Turn here. No, the second turn off the roundabout. I think we've gone too far – but look! This pub is adorable. Let's stop here." And we would. We had nowhere to be – and no car seat in the back. So we'd linger over a pint or two and wonder what the rest of our day – and days might bring.

When Erin and her three younger brothers entered the picture in surprisingly quick succession, copilot duties expanded to keeping the little people fed and happy. While the boys can now pretty much manage this on their own, Erin still requires close surveillance – which adds to the allure of driving. More in sync with her moods and preferences, I'm frequently in the hot seat, but I find it a welcome and admittedly amusing switch to see Bill take my place.

When Erin wakes, he parcels out the contents of the *Happy Meal* one by one, including a stuffed, unidentifiable object from the movie, *Soul*. He contorts to clean the ketchup from her face, fingers, and chair while she fires off requests for her favorite songs. "*Dynamite* by BTS, Dad! *American Girl! Let it Go!*" Bill scans my phone for her selections. Struggling, he tries to distract by pointing out a *Target* truck. He proposes we switch seats. I decline.

Eventually, though, we must stop, get gas and trade places. I dole out popcorn and Peanut M&Ms as we begin to make up time in the Carolinas. I start to doze off listening to Bill pepper Erin with questions about the *Puppy Dog Pals* and passing cars. She tugs on my shoulder every few minutes to ensure we are both fully alive and engaged – and the snacks have not run dry.

We couldn't be further from the English countryside and an impromptu pub lunch. I wish we could pay those two kids a visit, pull up a chair and order a pint. I'm not sure where I'd begin or whether any of this should be shared. I guess I'd just tell them to turn up the volume while they can, switch seats every now and then, and enjoy the ride.

"God made the world round so we would
never be able
to see too far down the road."

Isak Denisen

Surviving a Special Needs Marriage

When Erin turned 13, I wanted to hit the pause button. Seeing her body outgrow her mind terrified me. As my marriage approaches its 18th year ("almost an adult," a friend noted), a part of me feels the same way. We've made it through our fair share of "for better or worse." Who wants to "grow up" and see what "sickness and health" lay ahead? Let's just stay here. Sometimes I look back on those two people exchanging vows on a late September afternoon and can't help but think how naïve they were.

As all seasoned couples know, standing before your friends and family promising, with whatever words you choose, to stick by this person in good times and bad – you really have no idea what you're agreeing to. They are just words, and you have to say them to make it official and to get on with the party. This is not to say you don't mean them. But you simply cannot know how to love someone in good times and in bad until you are muddling through hell with them. Who can know what better or worse means when your greatest concern at the moment is making it down the aisle without tripping?

Three months after our wedding, those words manifested in a move to a foreign city in the middle of a very dark winter. Shortly after, a miscarriage morphed into months and then years of trying to have a baby. "Maybe it's not meant to be – it's fine, we're ok" – and then the "for better" appeared – a baby, a girl.

Soon enough, wow, a second – that was fast! How'd that happen? Life is good – two kids – a girl and a boy – fancy that – who would have thought? Then a diagnosis and the "for worse" comes into play – developmental delays, cognitive and motor impairments, sensory issues. I soon realized the hardest thing that has ever happened to me was also happening to someone else, someone with an exceptionally kind and patient heart – but who is different than I in many ways.

Differences aside, we had to figure out how to carry this thing together without dropping it or breaking it or shattering ourselves in the process. Sometimes we hand it off to each other. Often I am the one diving in – reading the books, meeting the teachers and specialists. It's easy to feel like I'm carrying it alone.

But when I need him to be there, he shows up. He cancels meeting and rearranges travel when I can't see one more doctor or therapist alone – when I need someone to witness the raised eyebrows, the somber, apologetic, or brusque tones – he is there.

Even then though I don't always let him off the hook – largely because I am profoundly sad (and exhausted) and it feels like the only thing I can do with this sadness is to hand it off to him in the form of anger – anger at him for not being around enough, for having to take off so soon when he does show up, for getting us into this predicament in the first place – because obviously the whole thing is his fault. In those early years a good deal of irrationality entered the picture as we processed the fact that things had turned out so very differently than planned, though we had not planned anything at all.

We thought we'd get married, have a kid or two or three and deal with the usual bruises, breaks, scrapes, and stitches. We knew in theory there would be larger things. We all know they're out there but they don't enter the picture when you're standing on that altar or holding your newborn. You and your husband are so incredibly capable of making this work – of protecting them. Nothing is going to touch them – nothing you won't be able to fix with a glass of water, a band-aid or maybe a quick trip to the ER. We'll be back on to the "for better" before we know it. It doesn't work like that. We all know this.

We knew it, too, deep down. We were not new to the world when we made those vows. But maybe that's the beauty of a couple speaking those words in a suspension of disbelief – a willingness to put on hold what you know to be true.

About two years into having kids – shortly after Erin's diagnosis – Bill took to checking in daily to ask: "So what's the crisis of the day?" I never fail to deliver. Some are small – we can't find the pink tie-dye shirt and she refuses to get dressed without it. Some are larger, like the other day when she put her fist through a window in a post-seizure haze.

That's what makes a special needs marriage – any marriage – work. Understanding and accepting that sometimes it just doesn't. Adapting to a constant redefinition of terms, of words, of good days and what constitutes a crisis for better or worse. You have to realize that while you said you'd love this person no matter what, some days there's no love left in the tank.

And that's ok – as long as you hold on to the understanding that you committed to not just words but a process, a work in progress, and that though tomorrow will not be without its chaos and crisis it may indeed hold a for better or two as well.

"I tell you this
to break your heart,
by which I mean only
that it break open, and never close again
to the rest of the world."

Mary Oliver
"Lead"
New and Selected Poems Volume Two

Seizures and Silver Linings

Erin developed epilepsy at age 13. There are no positives, but as they have become part of our reality and our routine – or part of what throws it off – I've come to find an upside.

When I shared this thought with a friend she asked, "Exactly what *upside* pops to mind?"

While it may sound cliché to make or find the best of a bad situation, to turn those lemons into lemonade, the reality is, what choice do I have?

There is no predicting when a seizure will occur. They seem to have no rhyme or reason. There are certain factors that can contribute to them – sleep deprivation, dehydration, constipation – but largely it's out of our control.

I learned early on, like most parents, how little control I have over our children's movements. They roll, they crawl, they pull to stand and they're off testing limits. At 12 months my oldest son stumbled into a coffee table requiring what seems the rite of passage ER visit and eyebrow stitch. At age 2, my second guy swallowed a bright pink ball of Borax based putty. Poison control was not amused. And when it comes to my youngest, a preemie prone to chest infections, my husband and I logged countless hours in a steam shower willing croup away.

As parents, we do everything we can to ward away bad and harmful things. We pad, secure, and buckle them in. We dispense the antibiotics and chicken soup. We cheer on their small bodies – but deep down we know it's out of our hands.

Seizures hammer that lesson home with a mallet. When something takes hold of your child from within, terror grips you to the core. I have never felt so helpless as I did watching Erin's fingers and lips turn blue during her first grand-mal. I was convinced we were going to lose her and there was not one thing I could do about it.

I turned her on her side. She continued to convulse. I prayed for it to stop but could not stop thinking, *so this is how it ends*. After what felt like an hour later (probably closer to two minutes), she stopped shaking and her breathing returned to normal. Were she not lying in a bathtub, she looked as though she were napping.

SEIZURES AND SILVER LININGS

What I thought was the end was really just the beginning of a new chapter. A harrowing introduction to our "new normal." Over the years we've learned to navigate an ever-shifting terrain of unexpected behaviors, calls, reactions to medications and social situations. Really the only thing we know to expect is the unexpected.

Children condition parents to adopt this mind frame. Kids don't always conform to a schedule. They don't move as fast or as fluidly as we would like. They don't sleep, they refuse to get dressed, they have meltdowns and bloody noses just as you're racing out the door. You miss the bus, the class, the appointment, the party. Miss after miss though you realize it doesn't matter.

At the same time, perspective can be hard to come by as a parent. A friend's son recently lost a middle school championship basketball game and he, the dad, was bereft. He understood that this was a completely irrational response, but parenthood can be a very irrational endeavor.

When you have a child, you are handed a stranger for whom you would lay down your life and whose emotions will always serve as a barometer for your own. Their arrival establishes a new world order. It's as if that baby comes with a camera lens which zooms in and pans out over and over again: we can control everything. We can control nothing.

The very definition of a good day transforms. What it means to be happy, what we value and prioritize shifts. Life itself takes on new meaning because you are responsible for keeping another person alive.

The onset of Erin's seizures forced us to slow down, to take it one moment at a time, to see every seizure free day as a small victory – and to appreciate how very fortunate we are to be alive today.

Epilepsy was not categorized as a neurological disorder until the mid-19th century. Historically it was considered "The Sacred Disease" because the afflicted were thought to be invaded by demons or evil spirits. If we lived at another time, Erin would be looked upon with suspicion, treated as a social outcast. With understanding and knowledge comes acceptance and for that I am grateful.

More so I am thankful that medicine has helped to reign in her seizures. They now occur less frequently and have been limited to the lesser: petit mal. This is not the case for all.

Just a few days ago I heard that a friend's 19-year-old daughter passed away after living with a life-long seizure condition. My heart broke for all this mom had been through. Surely there is no positive to any of this, I thought, reeling it all back – until I found myself sitting in a packed church listening to that mom deliver a eulogy about silver linings.

She spoke with passion and grace about the many lessons her daughter taught her. While her daughter could not talk and could not walk, she could love, and she could smile. "She had a beautiful smile," she said through tears and a smile of her own. Her daughter redefined happiness and hope for all who knew her and for that her mom was grateful.

Her joy and gratitude reminded me that whatever life hands us, we can hold, care for and enjoy our children and each other as long as we can. We can't control the when and why or how, but we can react with strength and love. Maybe that's the upside, the silver lining.

"Be patient toward all that is unsolved
in your heart
and try to love the questions themselves..."

Rainer Maria Rilke
Letters to a Young Poet

Relying on Science, Going on Faith

Since Erin's diagnosis, I have relied on science to guide us through our days. Without science I don't know where we would be. At the same time, many days leave me with more questions than answers. Without faith and a willingness to embrace the questions and believe that some mysteries will always remain, I would be lost.

We have worked with a host of therapists and medical professionals to address Erin's physical, mental and emotional challenges. One doctor in particular has served as a consistent touchstone along this journey. A highly regarded neurologist, he sees possibilities in Erin many do not and strives to tease that potential from her and us.

"I know she's capable of more," he says looking beyond whatever crisis we hand him. His conviction and optimism surprise me. I don't know what he bases it on – aside from a glimmer in her eye, her attention to detail, a hunch? So often he seems to go with his gut. "I have a good feeling about this," he said the other day, as we mapped out a new approach to a recent bout of aggression.

We have recently been mired in a ten-month cycle of extremely challenging behaviors. When I asked our doctor why several trials of new medications had failed and why the old ones had lost their efficacy, his answer surprised me.

"You know humans are always looking for answers," he said. "That's what makes us human – and solves a lot of questions, by the way. But we frustrate when we can't find the answers and ... maybe that's where faith and religion come in."

He could probably tell that his words took me off guard, sounding more preacher than pediatrician. In the same breath he assured me that they were not meant as a white flag and that he would never stop working toward an answer: "I will never say I don't have another idea."

As much as I appreciated his commitment to helping our daughter, I found surprising comfort in his admission that sometimes answers elude and that sometimes we must, as the poet Rilke wrote: "Live the questions." His willingness to acknowledge this made me realize that like the rest of us, doctors and scientists often reside in a space between questions and answers, a place often reserved for poets and prophets.

Scientists spend hours, days and years researching ideas, testing theories, and running trials. Each requires a small leap of faith. In many ways their profession is not much different from that of parenting.

The decision to parent a child requires one to marry the principals of the scientific method: observation, experiment, testing and modification of hypotheses with the art of living with uncertainty, letting go and relying on faith. However many years under the belt, regardless of a child's abilities, parents most often inhabit a space between questions and answers, a space where science ends and hope begins. It's not always an easy or comfortable space, but we hang on to faith as it's the only alternative.

My son recently got his driver's permit. He wants to jump behind the wheel every chance he can. My knee jerk is to keep him in the passenger seat. Will he be ok out there on the road? I hope, but I know that this is a hope grounded in reason: hours and hours of practice.

One hand instinctively on the dashboard, I remind him to use the blinker, to slow down, to focus on the intersection ahead and not the music. I point out the obvious, a stop sign, a truck double parked, a woman walking her dog just up the road. As we roll along, I forget to worry for a minute, glance out the window and continue on faith.

"Always be on the lookout for wonder."

E.B. White

Finding Awe in the Every Day

A few years ago I took a video of Erin gazing at Christmas lights. She was 15-years-old but marveled as if she were seeing them for the first time: "Oooooh! They are so beautiful. Look at the lights. They are awesome!"

Erin approaches life with uninhibited exuberance. While I have spent much of the past two decades trying to pull her out of her own world, she has worked equally hard to pull me into hers, imploring me to see life from a perspective filled with wonder. However rushed we may be, Erin demands that we take the time to appreciate and admire the sun shining, the birds "tweeting," and the "beautiful, red sweater" the bus driver is wearing today.

Dacher Keltner, a psychologist at Cal Berkley, explores how this emotion Erin comes by so naturally can positively impact our health and well-being. "The experience of awe helps us get out of our own heads and realize our place in the larger context," writes Keltner in: *Awe: The New Science of Everyday Wonder and How It Can Transform Your Life*.

Keltner defines awe as: "The feeling of being in the presence of something vast, something that transcends our understanding of the world." But he is quick to qualify that it's also simpler than we think. While the Northern Lights will certainly inspire awe, so can a child's artwork or the arc and swish of a three-point-play. Like Erin we can all find moments of awe in the everyday - a sunset, a song, a small gesture of kindness or humility.

We don't have to travel far to experience moments of awe. I am amazed by groups of local high school students who run food and clothing drives for the homeless, neighbors who band together to help those in crisis, as well as the steadfast presence of our school crossing guards ensuring safe passage for all.

I am consistently awed by moments of exceptional consideration my daughter elicits. Neighbors and shop keepers go out of their way to brighten her day, librarians welcome her like an old friend, while countless cashiers at any number of local businesses look up, startled and smile when she asks: "What's your name?" Erin inspires so many to pause, to see and to move beyond themselves. And when they do, my gratitude knows no bounds.

While there are plenty of moments in which I wish she would conform a little more readily to social norms, like practicing voice modulation in small spaces, Erin's lack of self-consciousness, attention to detail, curiosity and unceasing search for and ability to create moments of awe is one behavior I strive to emulate.

"Moments of awe quiet the self-critical voice of our self or ego and empower us to open our minds to wonder," writes Keltner. "They humble and remind us we are a small part of a larger whole. Some inherently know this."

I recently asked a beloved physician in our community if I could write a profile about her to spotlight the positive impact she makes on so many lives. "Thank you, I appreciate it, but no," was the reply.

Wow, this struck me. In the age of selfies and Tik Tok fame, I was bowled over by this whisper of humility. I felt a bit like Willy Wonka when Charlie returns a small piece of candy: "So shines a good, in this case, humble, deed – in a weary world."

Our world is no less weary than Charlie's. We are not lacking for reasons to worry. But as Erin and experts agree, there is a panacea: slow down, pay attention, allow yourself to look and to listen to the kid inside or next to you ask: "What's your name?" or simply exclaim: "Wow, that is awesome!"

"All grown-ups were once children – but only a few of them remember it."

Antoine de Saint-Exupery
The Little Prince

*

"What if Christmas, he thought, doesn't come from a store. What if Christmas...perhaps... means a little bit more!"

Dr. Seuss
How the Grinch Stole Christmas.

Finding Joy in Aisle Nine

Late November the weight of anticipation begins to grow. It's hard to shake the feeling that there's something we should be doing, something we should be planning or purchasing and a host of special events of which we should be apart. While an onslaught of holiday songs and commercials will have us believe everyone is doing something fun and magical, it's easy to forget that fun and magical means something different to everyone.

"Do you think we'd try *The Nutcracker* with Erin this year?" my mom asked the other day. Over the years we have taken Erin on many holiday outings yet as the question hung in the air it was evident we had forgotten this and taken a moment to indulge in an alternate holiday reality.

Dressed in festive apparel we float down city sidewalks admiring the glimmering lights and jubilant sounds which are loud and bright yet do not trigger any sensory issues. It's neither cold nor wet nor windy. No pressing crowds. No lines. No unforeseen delays. We make our way seamlessly to the theater and the seats which are neither too close nor too far away from the stage. Erin sits serenely for the duration of the performance. She is not freaked out by the army of gigantic mice or startled by the pop of the Toy Soldier's toy gun. She does not stand up and announce that she is "DONE" in the middle of the Dance of the Sugar Plum Fairies and does not beeline back to her happy place: the concessions stand where I am not dripping in sweat and chocolate having chased her up the aisle and pried a gigantic Hershey Bar from her vice like grip.

"I think it might be a lot," I said.

My mother, whose thought bubble likely imploded at the same time, agreed as we headed out to the store. Half-joking I suggest we're probably safer sticking with *Stop 'n Shop* and reminded Erin to bring the grocery list.

Holding fast to a crumpled piece of yellow paper, Erin methodically checked off each item. Aisle by aisle we filled the cart with bananas and broccoli, cereal and snacks. Some favorites: raisin bread. Some surprises: popcorn in a purple bag! "Ice Cream and Desserts" brought on some heated negotiations, and we paused for a round of karaoke in "Prepared Foods" where Erin jumped up and down belting out Ed Sheeran's *Castle on the Hill* playing on the speakers above. Though we lost a container of pineapples at checkout, everything else Erin placed not always so gently on to the conveyer belt and into a bag made it home unscathed.

"That was awesome!" Erin said as we exited the store. And it was. It was the height of ordinary, or our ordinary - and it was divine. A perfectly timed reminder that sometimes that is all you need.

This is not to sound bah-humbug. I love the holidays. Erin *really* loves the holidays. Sometimes though it's ok to dial it down, to remember the joy that can be found in everyday outings, in hearing a favorite song in aisle nine, in preparing and sharing a meal or reading something that makes you smile.

It can be hard to ward off December's pull and pressure to create, to do and to document something special, something spectacular. And this is not to say these things should not be done. "These things are good, these things are fun!" writes Dr. Suess. As Erin reminds me at every turn though, it's the joy you derive in the doing that matters most.

This holiday season whether the doing entails travel to Lincoln Center, London or the living room if it makes you happy, if it makes your kid smile, if it makes anyone say: "That was awesome!" be grateful and know that it really is just that.

"And whether or not it is clear to you, no doubt the universe is unfolding as it should...Therefore, be at peace with God, whatever you conceive him to be. And whatever your labors and aspirations in the noisy confusion of life, keep peace in your soul...Strive to be happy."

Max Ehrmann
Desiderata

Thirteen

"Does Erin know what it means to be a teenager?" a friend asked.

"I think so – but I'm not really sure," I said.

Erin knows that 13 is not 12 – nor is it 14. Whether she understands that 13 is "greater than" or "less than" either is unclear to me. She is not good with numbers. I've never been much of a number's person either, though I have come to understand that some numbers hit harder than others.

When you have a developmentally disabled child, a part of you does not want them to grow up. Watching their body outgrow their mind and ability to reason brings with it a terror all its own. You want to push the pause button – or better yet, rewind.

When they are young a lot of behaviors can be passed off as simply part of the terrain of being just what they are, young. The meltdowns and sudden swings of emotion in public spaces can easily be passed off as "normal" when they are small enough to be picked up and whisked away, out of ear and eyeshot. But now, Erin is stronger than I am. She can no longer be quickly removed in what we had perfected as our ongoing series of "nothing to see here" moves.

These days when things are not going our way there is a lot – and a lot of her – to see. We attempt reasoning, then bribing (no library, if…) to get her out of certain situations. Sometimes when we are in a store, she will spot, swipe or hold with a vice like grip any number of random objects – be it a rubber yellow duck, a stuffed Elmo, or a King Kone ice cream. Contrary to most behavior therapists' advice, generally we just buy the coveted item and move along thereby averting a public tantrum. At home we have a mountain of stuffed animals we have purchased to literally "buy" our way out of sticky situations. Maybe we should care less about what the person on line behind us thinks – but we are human, as are Erin's younger brothers. Sometimes if the only path to momentary peace in all forms is an 18th copy of *Clifford the Big Red Dog*, you just go with it.

As the years pass and Erin more closely resembles the adult she will one day be, it's been difficult not to imagine what the future may hold – where she will live, who will care for her, who will love her. Shortly after we learned about Erin's condition, I asked a doctor what we could do to help her. In addition to a variety of therapies he said: "I would suggest you have more children – so there is someone to take care of her – when you are gone."

My husband and I were not in the same place when we received her diagnosis. He had returned to New York, where he was starting a new job when the geneticist called to discuss the results. Bill, as stoic as they come, walked to a small park on First Avenue, sat on a bench, and cried – crushed under the weight of a dramatically altered future for his daughter and the prospect of calling to inform his wife of this swift and sudden change of course.

Though deep down we had a feeling something was *not right* as Erin began to fall behind the first year's milestones, we were both living with the "outside of normal" assessment a neurologist had offered a few months earlier. With a child of 22 months, with any child, you're often just shooting for normal: walking, talking, school, sports, friends – or what, at the time, you figure is the natural progression. Up until that point we had a hazy image of what the future would hold. It was pretty typical and typical looked good.

In the months and years to come we combed the city looking for direction. I remember remarking to one doctor that I thought it strange that he had not seen any patients with this disorder. "Well, most people here (as if I were from another planet) do prenatal screenings and terminate should anything appear abnormal," he said, (scoring an all-time low on the bedside manner chart.)

There's a reason for such high rates of divorce in the special needs community. A disabled child takes a formidable toll on a marriage – physically, emotionally, financially. Bill and I are fortunate to have an exceptional network of friends and family to fall back on and still it is not easy. While we are blessed in many ways and grateful that Erin is engaged and happy, her diagnosis terminated many of the unspoken hopes we had for our daughter. And how a couple processes that and confronts the unique challenges that it entails is something no support system, however wide or deep, can ever really answer.

For much of Erin's first few years, my father-in-law a hard charging businessman who tried hard to understand the extent of her disability and how he could help would consistently ask: "What I'd like to know is will she one day be able to walk down the street and buy herself a cup of coffee?" I never really had an answer for him as

THIRTEEN

he passed away when Erin was nine-years-old. But I now know it is unlikely.

With all the uncertainty that Erin's and our future holds what I do know is that as she has grown so has her exuberance for the most seemingly mundane particulars of life. Little kids jump up and down all the time at the thought of ice cream or a toy store. So does Erin. She is five foot five inches tall and still jumps and claps at the sight of her favorite places or people. "Look Mom, a book store!" Or: "Here is grandma," she shouts – and bounds into her arms.

Erin is joyful. Though her body has begun to change and puberty is upon us, she is very much a child and not saddled with teenage angst or attitude. She does not use sarcasm – figurative language alone perplexes and amazes: "Your head is going to blow up?" she echoes after I have overreacted to something generally involving her brothers. "No, Erin, it's not really going to blow up. That just means I am frustrated."

As the unanswerable questions have piled up over the years, what I do know today is that I have a teenager who shares my passion for books and music. Who loves ice cream and chocolate chip cookies, pancakes, bananas, and blueberries. Who waxes poetic at the "dancing trees" blowing in the wind yet does not know that 45 is older than 37. Who is more affectionate and effusive than I – and most people I know. Who loves and hugs unconditionally and brings smiles to all who cross her path. Erin lives in the moment and the moments with her are good. There's something to be said for that.

And whether she knows what it is to be a teenager, she knows what it is to be happy – and she knows what makes her smile. Not a lot of teenagers – not a lot of people – do. For Erin it's very simple. Her nursery rhyme books, her dog Pablo, her friend Catherine and her family gathered around to sing and to help blow out the candles – all 13.

"I've learned that people will forget what you said, people will forget what you did, but people will never forget how you made them feel."

Maya Angelou

Losing Pop-Pop

Every time my mother arrives at our house Erin asks: "Where's Pop-pop?"

She knows the answer but craves the exchange and its subject. They both do.

"Oh Erin, you know," my mother replies. "Where is Pop-pop?"

"He's in heaven," Erin answers.

I don't know if Erin knows what the answer means. I am not sure I do either, but it's something she feels she must ask if only to convey that she's thinking about him. Erin often asks questions in an effort to make a statement, express a desire or share an emotion.

Until recently Erin had seldom seen my mom without my dad. No one had. They went together like Ernie and Bert, Anna and Elsa and all the other logical pairs in Erin's life. For her and the rest of us, the singularity of my mother's presence is striking. Something is missing and Erin notes the absence with a question and their well-rehearsed script.

Unlike the boys who feel that mentioning my dad might make my mom sad or remind her that he is no longer here, Erin plows right through. She really knows no other way to be. As the rest of us wade through grief in our own way, I've begun to feel that maybe what has been labeled as an "impaired" way of being is less a "deficit" and more a strength, at least when it comes to processing the death of someone you love.

My father had an aggressive form of Dementia called Lewy Body Disease, which took its toll in progressive stages: hallucinations, irritability, forgetfulness. A lifelong teacher, in later stages, he often mistook my brothers for bus drivers and colleagues and my sons for former students. While he never forgot the love he felt for my mom, his wife of 51 years, there were moments when my mother, sister and I were interchangeable.

He never, however, forgot Erin and their relationship never missed a beat. She did not know he was losing hold of his world. She only knew that she loved him and that they loved so many of the same things: car rides, country music, comfort food.

My dad always embraced Erin's difference and as the disease progressed, their connection only seemed to intensify. Big on hugs and squeezes, Erin is a tactile communicator. She hugged my dad a lot and he, never a big talker, hugged her back hard.

She, unlike the rest of us, never grew impatient with his increasingly quirky behaviors. She didn't object to his opening and closing the front door fifty times a day. She saw no issue in his pouring ketchup on his pancakes. She did not mind that he sometimes walked in circles in our driveway and asked repeatedly to go for a drive.

Erin also finds great satisfaction in closing open cabinets, drawers, and bottle caps. She follows no hard and fast rules when it comes to food consumption. And she understands that sometimes a walk or a drive to no place in particular is just what you need.

Erin visited my dad in hospice care at his home. She crawled on to the bed beside him and rubbed his arm – two bodies always on the go joined in an unfamiliar but content stillness. "Pop-pop is sleeping," she said quietly and stared at him as if in a trance.

In the moments Erin has seen me upset about my father's death, she asks: "Are you sad?" She knows what sadness is; for her I believe she feels it most in the absence of their affectionate exchange. She seems to process this by conjuring his memory in the mundane moments she shared with him.

"Pop-pop likes this song."

"Pop-pop likes sweet potatoes."

"Pop-pop likes blueberry pie."

Like many who live with neurological disorders, Erin does not use the past tense. I start to correct her: "Yes he likes – actually, he liked – okay, fine, he likes."

Erin communicates as she lives, only in the present and implores all around her to do the same.

Erin did not attend the funeral. It would have been unfair to demand that she sit in a wooden pew and listen to unfamiliar faces lecture about life and love. She would have asked to leave with my mom and go to a bookstore. She would have wanted my undivided attention, while I had to deliver a eulogy in which I talked about Erin and my dad and how he never considered her to be "impaired" or to have a "disability." He thought she was bright, brilliant, and funny.

"She doesn't miss a trick," he'd often say.

I think he's right.

"Change. But start slowly,
because direction
is more important than speed."

Paulo Coehlo

A Time to Grow

There's a tree outside my window that has yet to shed its leaves. I've been concerned since last fall. I don't know what this means for the spring. I worry but understand its reluctance to let go as this has been topic number one in our home over the past few months.

Erin recently aged out of a school for teens with special needs and started a program for young adults. She didn't want to leave her teacher and her friends. She has been asking every day to see them and to go back.

Erin, 21, could go to school forever. Part of me wishes we could make this happen. She thrives and finds comfort in a predictable and happy routine: Morning Meeting, Story Time, Arts and Crafts, Snack, Music, Community Outings.

We've talked a lot about how hard it is to leave a place and people that you love. I've explained that her brother who left for college last September loved his school too and did not want to leave his friends but that it was time for him to discover new places and people and do new and exciting things.

She is not heartened by this story. Erin would prefer to remain unchanged. She loved her cozy classroom and the intimacy of the setting. It was warm, familiar, and comfortable. I shared her hesitation. I've felt this way as each of my children have moved through their milestones, nostalgia tinged with a sense of trepidation and the inevitable: 'Oh boy, what next!?'

But I know even if she could have stayed in school forever eventually I would have worried. I had already been wondering was she being challenged enough, was she working to meet her potential. What is her potential? I have no idea, but I believe she has more in there and the capacity to understand and experience the world in a deeper way. And I know the only way we can discover this is to move on, to step outside and to see what becomes of feeling uncomfortable this time.

The day we received Erin's diagnosis a doctor gave us our marching orders. He mentioned Early Intervention and noted that with intensive therapy 'some kids' show 'some improvement' but we had to get on it. Erin, then

22 months, wanted no part of therapists making demands on her time and redirecting her from preferred activities like loading and unloading a toy box. But gradually she got on board and gained skills I never thought possible.

So, we dove in and found the specialists, the schools, the programs that worked until they didn't and then started all over again. There have been so many settings in which I wanted Erin to remain forever. Time after time, though, one after the other, magically new and exceptional programs and people appeared.

Maybe this is why I am so troubled by our tree holding fast to its dried brown leaves through snow and ice, wind and rain while all her tree friends stand majestically bare, branches outstretched, waiting for that not long off day when it's time to grow again. I don't want her to miss out on the magic. I want us all to see and understand the good and the beauty to be found in letting go.

"Your children are not your children.
They are the sons and daughters of life's
longing for itself.
They come through you but not from you.
And though they are with you yet they
belong not to you.
You may give them love but not your thoughts,
For they have their own thoughts.
You may house their bodies but not their souls.
For their souls dwell in the house of tomorrow,
Which you cannot visit, not even in your dreams.
You may strive to be like them, but
Seek not to make them just like you.
For life goes not backward, nor tarries
with yesterday."

Kahil Gibran
"On Children"
The Prophet

Point to Happy

This summer a friend asked if Erin understands that her brother is leaving for college. Erin's grown accustomed to the comings and goings of her brothers. Covid's quarantines conditioned us all to endure long absences, but this has thrown us both for a loop.

Raising a child with autism requires a fair amount of explaining and interpreting the world. When Erin was younger we often read a book called *Point to Happy*, which connected emotion with experience. In my efforts to prep her on the details of this most recent milestone I feel like an unreliable narrator. I know she senses my unease and at times not sure who's leading who through this transition.

Erin taught herself to read by memorizing the shape and sounds of letters and then words. In much the same way she recalls the answers to certain questions. Her address. The name of her town. She knows what to say when asked where Will is going to school.

I don't know if she understands what that means but the repetition helps. Eventually it just becomes what is.

I think it helps both of us as I often find myself joining her in this exercise to make what's new and different just part of the norm. Will is leaving which is great but in some ways hard. And his older sister is staying which is also great but in other ways hard.

We gather the linens, the laundry bin, the desk lamp. The whole thing is nothing short of amazing. The little boy who two minutes ago was swinging upside down in the park can now make his bed, sort his clothes and dress himself. As hard as it is to see him leave home, I am grateful that he can go. Point to happy. Point to sad. Point to anxious.

With all that's going on in the world and the many challenges I see Erin face just getting through her day, it seems small minded to allow anything but joy enter this picture. I am not sending my son off to war. We are blessed by a multitude of riches: food, shelter, clothing, a country when not at odds with itself is largely at peace.

But even so, leave taking involves risk. We're reminded every day. Even in the best of times and the most ideal of conditions, safe return is not guaranteed. My freshman year of college a close friend's mom got that call, just a few days after Thanksgiving, just a stone's throw to Christmas.

A slick road. A car failed to negotiate a turn. We had all just gathered days before.

I know this is not the norm, this was an exception. Yet, exceptional things happen every day. Often exceptionally beautiful – which Erin never fails to point out. Sunshine is cause for celebration and must not be overlooked.

This morning's sky for the first time in a while was gray. "Where is the sun hiding?" Erin asked looking out her bedroom window. *It's behind the clouds today, but it's out there.* From the moment she was born Erin has required that I hold her close, that I think about, study and see what I might have missed.

Erin attends a life and job skills training program. When not "frustrated" or "disappointed" by a change in schedule, she is mostly happy. She has taught me so much about life, love and persevering. Against all odds, she learned to walk, to talk and to connect with the world around her. Sometimes I think she understands and relates better than anyone I've ever known – to people, to me, to her brother, her first friend, playmate, and protector.

Every night Erin watches the same movie: *Homeward Bound*, a story about three beloved pets who get separated from their family. Lost in the Oregon wilderness, they face tremendous obstacles, a bobcat, an icy mountain range, a battering storm, but every night they find their way back home. Erin delights in the miracle of their return and though I've seen it play out one hundred times before I can't help but applaud alongside her.

She is full of joy and every step of the way helps me to see that she and her brother are each moving in the direction of a life unfolding uniquely for them, to appreciate that they are both working hard to meet new and formidable challenges, to believe that whether it's the end of the day or the end of a semester they will find their way back home – and above all, to celebrate that return, preferably with applause.

"How lucky I am to have something that makes saying goodbye so hard."

A.A. Milne
Winnie the Pooh

On Losing a Good Dog

Three weeks after Pablo died Erin finally said: "Pablo's not coming back." The days after his passing were filled with questions: "When can we pick him up?" "When will Pablo come home?" It's hard for anyone to imagine life without their first love, for Erin it was impossible.

Pablo, a Black Lab with caramel colored eyes, joined our family when Erin was nine and he was three. He had velveteen ears, a white patch on his chest and a significant drooling problem. I had never owned a dog before and couldn't help but ask the trainer who placed him with us: "Is that normal?" As it turns out it's not, but Pablo was not a normal dog.

Pablo was a service dog trained to help children with autism and their families. While her three brothers grew to adore him, Pablo was Erin's dog. He was charged with keeping her safe and happy.

As a child Erin had a tendency to wander. I had lost her on more than one occasion. It happens in a blink – in the time it takes to reach for a bunch of bananas, to feed a parking meter or to pick up a younger sibling. A mere glimpse of something enticing and they are gone.

Tethered to Erin by a lead attached to his bright blue vest, Pablo was trained to bolt in place if he felt her stray. At the same time, when Pablo moved in a certain direction, Erin knew to follow. Holding fast to his harness, Erin regularly walked the two miles from our house to the library their home away from home.

Upon reaching their destination he'd sit beside her for as long as it took to find just the right book, often stretching out knowing it could take a while. Every visit the librarians greeted the duo by name, while, Patrick, the owner of our local bookstore always offered treats and pretended to look away as Pablo closely inspected boxes of books lining the floor - a formidable strand of saliva dangling precariously close to the covers.

Customers frequently stopped to engage Erin and her gentle guide, allowing her to see beyond herself, to be seen and to interact with those around her. Pablo both grounded and heightened Erin's senses and ability to relate to others.

Most profoundly he bolstered her sense of self, of acceptance and of being loved. They shared an intensely affectionate relationship. He was direct with his wants and needs, no facial expressions or subtleties to decipher and Erin knew that whatever the day may bring, Pablo loved her. While her dad, brothers and I, as well as a host of therapists and teachers encouraged 'appropriate' behavior Pablo only wanted love - and half her hamburger.

Erin knew Pablo was *her* dog. She beamed when people stopped to admire him. Our boys loved it too. Behavioral challenges frequently attracted unwanted attention, making the most mundane of family outings a high stress affair. Pablo turned that equation upside down. Her brothers were so proud of him and so grateful that their sister had found such a fun and faithful friend.

To the boys' infinite delight, he once inspired an entire elementary class to cheer "Pablo! Pablo! Pablo!" through the halls of the Norwalk Aquarium and almost incited a monkey riot at the Palm Beach Zoo when a group of visitors turned their attention away from them and to this large, furry creature. Pablo never failed to command attention and spotlight when and where attention must be paid.

Moments before Erin had her first seizure, Pablo appeared uncharacteristically agitated, moving in circles at the entrance to the bathroom where she was playing in the tub. I remember wondering what he was doing as he squeezed past me to sit beside her, when Erin started to convulse. Pablo sat next to me as I started to freak out. He probably knew that was going to happen, that I would react the way I did, that she and everything would be ok but he waited it out beside me just to be sure.

Pablo always made sure we were all ok. He saw us through the highs, lows and doldrums of eleven years. He spoke the secret language of boys, playing ball for hours, content to sit and snuggle while watching the big game. He was a best friend with a bottomless appetite - always up for sharing a snack. Best of all he was safe haven and a no judgement zone. He didn't care if your shoes matched, if you played well or struck out, if you won or lost – just that you came home.

It gutted us all to see him slow down. In his final months he wrestled with dental issues and a skin condition. His hips grew weak and cataracts obstructed his vision. Most disconcertingly, *he* began to wander. He didn't know what he wanted or where he was supposed to be. He knew he was destined to keep on the go, to keep us safe and he knew he was failing.

We all did, except Erin.

ON LOSING A GOOD DOG

Erin never saw a problem. She just saw Pablo. Even in his last days when he could barely get up from his bed. She'd wish him good morning, bring him treats, sit beside him and tell him about her day. *See you in the morning Pablo*, she said every night.

She never anticipated a time he wouldn't be there, as much as we explained that Pablo was tired, that he needed to rest – these were not explicit enough terms, but as it turns out, none exist.

Erin does not know what dying means and for now heaven is just somewhere she wants to be to see Pablo. *He is in a good place, he is happy*, I tell her. *Maybe not as happy as he was with you*, I back track reading her face, *but he will be when he sees you again.*

I miss him too. He was a good dog. This she understands.

"There is
always light.
If only we're
brave enough
to see it.
If only we're
brave enough
to be it."

Amanda Gorman
"The Hill We Climb"

In the summer of 2020 gymnastics great, Simone Biles, surprised fans and sparked controversy worldwide when she withdrew from five event finals at the Tokyo Olympics citing mental health concerns.

Lessons on Winning and Living

As the pressures of competition and social media takes its toll on a growing number of athletes and they retreat from the limelight citing mental health concerns, I wish I could introduce them to a young woman who would understand and applaud the decision to take a time out. Erin has never heard of Simone Biles but she knows what it takes to practice self-care and to be happy.

When Erin was born in London twenty summers ago, I imagined that maybe someday she'd win Wimbledon. I grew up playing competitive tennis so it seemed an entertaining speculation. Little did I know how much she had to teach me about what it means to win.

Since she could hold a crayon, Erin has been practicing how to write her name. While it's still a work in progress and I have faith she will get there, over the years Erin has taught me that knowing how to write your name is not as important as knowing your name - and the names of the people you love.

When Erin meets someone named Tommy she lights up and says: 'We have a Tommy," referencing a much loved childhood friend who lives next door.

She's also eager to learn the names of all who cross her path. As she studies the person working the *Stop 'N Shop* checkout she never fails to ask: "What's your name?" Men and women on the other side of counters everywhere look up, somewhat perplexed, smile and say: "And what's yours?"

Erin knows her name. She knows what she likes, what she doesn't and where she wants to be. If the day is not going in the direction she likes, she has been known to stage a sit in. As much as this tactic drives me bonkers at times, I have come to admire her resolve and sense of purpose.

Erin has taught me if you are not happy with the moment, do whatever it takes to change it. She understands that when you are feeling sad or overwhelmed, it's ok to just sit on the stairs - *her* signature move.

As much as Erin inspires introspection, she's also taught me to embrace exuberance and spontaneity. She's taught me to celebrate the small things like hearing your favorite song at CVS. She's taught me to track the days by the people we might see and to mark the months by the birthdays and holidays they hold.

She's taught me it's ok to jump up and down when you are happy and there is no right or wrong time to hug someone you love. At one point, in an entirely pre-Covid exercise in personal space, Erin was given a 'hug schedule' at school. This made no sense to her and it did not last long.

I imagine much of the world does not make sense to Erin. She would never understand the fuss over anyone taking a step back from loud noise and bright lights. She watches her three younger brothers race to school and practice, their moods measured by wins, losses, scores and GPAs. She's never won a trophy. She has a few participation medals, which hold no weight to an outing with Grandma or sharing an ice cream with Pablo.

For Erin a trip to the library is a reason to smile, a win is time with someone you love and the stairs a steady refuge on a down day. Unless the All England Club instates an all tie-dye rule, Erin will never know or care about Wimbledon. My girl knows her stuff and she's taught me well.

"A little magic can take you a long way."

Roald Dahl
James and the Giant Peach

*

"Why sometimes I've believed as many as six impossible things before breakfast."

Lewis Carroll
Through the Looking Glass

Magical Thinking

Joan Didion wrote about a period of 'magical thinking' after her husband died. Her mind played tricks, convincing her at times that nothing had changed. Over the years I've engaged in my own more intentional magical thinking which has allowed me to catch my breath, to refocus and to appreciate what *is* rather than what might have been. Even on the worst of days, I have found, a small shift of perspective and mindset helps to ride the waves and process the enormity of all.

The other day I received a letter from our school district informing us that Erin will soon "age out" of state mandated educational services and requesting our attendance at a meeting to discuss the "transition to adulthood." While this is not news to me, seeing it officially documented makes it all the more real and harder to shelve - as I have been doing the past few months.

The concept of Erin "aging out" of anything is inconceivable to me. Erin approaches the world with a childlike curiosity and sense of wonder most people her age lost long ago. She goes to sleep every night anticipating the return of Mr. Golden Sun. Despite a deep devotion to her service dog, Pablo, her favorite book of the moment is *Pete the Cat*.

Erin has been at her current placement for two years. She loves her school, her teachers, and her routine. As we approach a precipice so many parents dread, due to a lack of ongoing services for young adults with special needs, I find myself reaching for some nonexistent pause button. I don't want to meet. I don't want to discuss. Instead, I'd like to believe that today is the only day we have to consider.

This is not the first time I've wanted to put time on hold and ignore a flurry of red flags ahead.

Well before we received Erin's diagnosis, I had a sense that something was lagging in her development - but it was easy to convince myself otherwise. She looked and acted like the other babies in our playgroup. Sure, her fine motor and self-soothing skills lagged a bit but at nine months no one is solving quadratic equations or dribbling a soccer ball. Erin could crawl around and put wayward objects in her mouth with the best of them. She was equally fascinated by picture books and brightly colored stuffed animals and her ability to sit spell bound through

MAGICAL THINKING

our *Mommy and Me* music classes rivaled any of her peers. So, I coasted - until I couldn't.

When we received Erin's diagnosis at 22 months and a geneticist detailed a host of delays and deficits, I found myself incapable of looking too far ahead. Instead, I resolved to take her home and take it one minute at a time. This urge to hyper focus on the present may be a knee jerk reaction to a daunting future, but it's also a lesson Erin has graced us with at every stage of her development: to slow down and focus on the now.

Erin has always required total attention - for safety's sake but also because she lives so fully in the moment. A short walk with her involves a requisite wave to our outsized shadows and a lengthy pause to admire the yellow daffodils. When I am with her the parameters of time and space and the harsher edges of reality slip away and it's easy to feel that all is well. We travel the same route to town as everyone else, just at a slower pace.

Alongside her younger brother Erin attended a mainstream preschool which she loved. With an aide by her side she joined in field trips, sat for circle time, and made holiday decorations. She did not converse or play 'typically' with other students, but the school provided a much needed 'typical' routine and the space for us to engage in some 'magical thinking' while we processed, adjusted, and tried to understand where we were going and what Erin needed.

As the years went by life provided other opportunities to coast and to focus solely on the moment at hand. We moved out of the city and Erin played in the backyard with the kids next door. Thanks to an exceptionally dedicated teacher she was able to thrive within a small self-contained classroom in one of our town's elementary schools. She and her classmates became part of the fabric of the community. Kids of all ages got to know her and to celebrate her and she had the chance to celebrate back.

As it tends to across the board, Middle School threw us some curve balls. Our town had no classroom or 'cohort:' a group of closely aged children of similar cognitive ability. So began years of musical schools, landing every now and then in a setting that worked for a limited time.

As we approach the end of another short but happy run and I'm forced to put an end to my latest round of magical thinking, I realize that if Erin and all these years have taught me nothing else it's that, good or bad, nothing lasts forever. And maybe just knowing that is magic enough.

"Enjoy the little things in life for one day you'll look back
and realize they were the big things."

Kurt Vonnegut

Celebrating the Small Things this Christmas

I watched the Rockefeller Christmas Tree lighting with my kids this week. As you would expect there were holiday songs and dancing, interspersed with commercials about the season and what to watch and buy.

"Christmas is here!" Al Roker announced.

On cue Erin sat up and asked when we were leaving for Grandma's house. "Not for a few weeks," I said, as my 9-year-old wondered how it could be snowing in the city when it was 50 degrees and raining at our house 30 minutes away.

Watching white flakes fall around a sparkling Sarah McLachlan, I explained that for some people snow means Christmas, but that *that* snow was not real. As I tried to prevent Erin from having a full-fledged meltdown because we were not immediately packing up to go over the river and through the woods, it felt as if the accelerated commercialization of Christmas and global warming had conspired to turn this short homework break into a panel discussion on climate change and the subjectivity of time.

I tried to play the role of wisdom-filled parent but understood their confusion. This time of year can feel like a fun house where nothing is at seems. Retailers will have you believe everyone is rushing to a fabulous party and time is moving at lightning speed.

"Act now! Buy now! Do not wait!"

As the weather remains temperate, the gradual climate shift only seems to compound the uncertainty. In our northeastern suburb it seems incongruous to haul gifts and evergreens over a doorstep full of fallen leaves. It's hard to usher in a new season when another refuses to leave.

This can be a bewildering time for anyone, let alone someone who has trouble conceptualizing the length of a day, a week or a month or understanding that however high those Rockettes kick we are not going to Grandma's now but instead four weeks from now. It's no easy lesson.

Over the years Erin has learned to use the traditional markers of time to give order to her days. The sun rises in the morning. Morning means raisin toast and the yellow bus. She thrives on routine, so we break her days into small increments. Every evening we write the next day and date on a white board and list the order of activities, including all minutiae: "Wake up, brush teeth, eat breakfast…" If she's going to do it, it's on there. She finds this an intensely grounding and joyful activity.

Through the repetition of this routine, she has memorized the joy certain days bring: Monday: music, Tuesday: cooking class, Wednesday: fit club. Similarly, she understands what to expect on holidays: Valentine's Day: hearts and chocolate (good,) Fourth of July: barbecues and fireworks (loud), and Christmas: Grandma's house (bliss.)

We celebrate Christmas at my parents' house and aside from her birthday it's Erin's favorite day of the year. My mom creates an evening that plays to all of Erin's strengths. There are stockings bulging with gifts, music, and stories read aloud. A Santa's helper even arrives with a sack full of toys. Each of my kids revels in every detail but Erin more than most – because Erin believes.

She delights in the magic of Christmas. She takes the holiday and much of life at face value and does not question the how or why of its traditions. Round man dressed in red, up and down the chimney. No problem.

Let's just be sure to leave him cookies and wish him well along the way.

What Erin does question is if Christmas is "here" and "now," why are we not "there?" Distraught by the reality, she spent the rest of that evening sitting on the stairs – her signature protest move. I empathize with her frustration.

I too find the season overwhelming and swing daily between denial and panic. *It can't be December; I don't even need a jacket. Oh my God did that woman just say she's finished with all her holiday shopping? What's wrong with people? What's wrong with me?* I fully understand Erin's inclination to plant herself on the staircase until she can wrap her head around the situation.

Sometimes I join her, and we just sit and listen to each other breathe – until we remember what helps get us moving again: the schedule. We pull out the white board and review what activities comprise tomorrow: dance class, a field trip to *Target,* a visit to our neighbor's house, and slowly a smile emerges. We've learned when you're caught in a tidal wave of a day or a week, sometimes the only way out is to live moment to moment and to focus on the routine – on the small things.

CELEBRATING THE SMALL THINGS THIS CHRISTMAS

Erin's hyper focus on routine tasks allows an intense recognition and appreciation of each and every minute. An uncanny focus on the present is what brings her joy – and every day brings its own set of magic and miracles. Erin has taught us to slow down and take the moments as they come, understanding that not unlike stepping-stones, if we get too far ahead we may slip and lose track of ourselves and time itself.

So, until it's time to leave for Grandma's house, we are going to drastically reduce TV time, keep our schedule close at hand and hold fast to the most essential details of our days: wake up, brush teeth, have breakfast, breathe.

"Real isn't how you are made.
It's a thing that happens to you.
When a child loves you for a long time,
not just to play with,
but REALLY loves you.
Then you become REAL."

Marjory Williams
The Velveteen Rabbit

Cookie Monster

This week Erin turns 16. Dressed in her favorite tie-dye shirt, she will open gifts of brightly colored stuffed animals and children's picture books. We will sing happy birthday and help her blow out her 16 candles. She will laugh and clap in joy – and I will smile, as I so often do when I am with her.

This was not always the case.

Shortly after we received Erin's diagnosis, Bill and I attended a conference for families living with this disorder. We were still reeling from the unexpected turn our lives had taken and the day's long lectures about what to expect and what the future would hold hit hard.

After watching a particularly disheartening (and dated) video about a seemingly punitive therapy called ABA – Applied Behavior Analysis, which had been suggested to us – we decided to call it a day and retreat to our hotel room.

As the elevator door opened, a large, teenage girl appeared cuddling a sizeable *Cookie Monster*. Beside her stood her mom, who ushered her out with a carefree smile – a smile that seemed to convey that this were the most normal scene in the world and there was not one thing wrong with this picture.

"Come on, Clare," her mom said.

Clare smiled, squeezed the bright blue monster and bounded through the elevator doors – thrilled with herself, her mom and whatever adventure that lay ahead – much the same way Erin does today.

My heart sank. I couldn't bear to think that this was where we were headed. Erin was still a baby – doing things that babies do. Though a little behind in her milestones, she was not yet expected to walk or talk or act "appropriately." She was prone to meltdowns, but she was entitled to them. After all she had teeth pushing through her gums – how could anyone keep it together with that happening? (Prior to her diagnosis, when I had no idea why she cried for hours and needed to be held 98 percent of the day, and night, I blamed most of it on teething.)

So she cried a lot and startled easily. Many babies do. The point is she was still a baby.

We were still working our way through the adorable outfits and gifts that had arrived shortly after her birth.

COOKIE MONSTER

As I watched Clare bounce off into the lobby, I pictured Erin in her tiny blueberry sundress with matching floppy hat and wanted to crumble.

We left the conference early and returned to the babies at home. We dove head first into Early Intervention and though I held it at bay for about nine months, eventually enlisted Erin in a 40-hour-per-week ABA program. We built a team of exceptionally dedicated therapists who rallied around and guided us through those early days.

As Erin grew I logged countless hours combing the city for sensory gyms, special needs activities, schools and specialists who could accommodate us. This was not the routine of a typical toddler. As the months and years passed though I grew less interested in what was "typical" and focused on what she needed.

Gradually I admitted to myself and everyone around me that the meltdowns were due less to teething and more to sensory and language deficits. I learned to accept and soon to embrace that my daughter experienced the world differently than most – and by extension, so did I.

It's a learning curve captured best in the essay and special needs parents' anthem: "Welcome to Holland." You planned a trip to Italy but ended up in Holland. You had long envisioned Tuscany's rolling hills, the Amalfi Coast and Coliseum. You ended up with tulips, windmills – and *Cookie Monster*. And while it's not a trip or story line you might have chosen, it's the one you're living. It's your story and the craziest part of the whole thing is the gratitude and wonder you begin to experience along this very unexpected journey.

Looking back I think I know why Clare's mom was smiling. She had walked far enough beside her daughter to find and to appreciate the rhythm. She had lived through enough bad days to know, however dark, they would be followed by good. She knew there were things far worse than having a teen who showers affection on all those she loves, moms and Muppets alike.

When those elevator doors opened at that conference, this lesson was still a ways off for me and fast forwarding 16 years was all too much. Comparing those freeze frames, I was missing the moments – all the days, hours and minutes that lead from a to z – the impossible and the miraculous, the setbacks and small victories, the kindness of doctors, therapists, friends and strangers who take the time to shape and mold my daughter and me into the pair we are today. One grateful mom and one tie dye clad teen clutching any one of *Sesame Street's* finest – full of joy.

"I do not understand the mystery of grace
– only that it meets us where we are
and does not leave us where it found us."

Anne Lamott

The Helpers

Parents of special needs children often hear: "Life or God doesn't give you anything you can't handle." Also: "You're so strong and such an amazing mom, this child was given to you for a reason." They are generally well-intentioned words and meant to help, but they don't, because as the years go by, you'll often feel that it's way more than you can handle, and you're really not that strong or amazing at anything.

The meltdowns and the sleepless nights will pile up, the behavior modification plan will go awry, and the experimental dietary restrictions will slide. Years of toilet training will feel like banging your head repeatedly against a wall. You will lose perspective and will think you are completely falling down on the job because you've been told life doesn't give you anything you can't handle.

And then one day you will hear your daughter's young therapist say to you: "I have a new idea." And you will look up and notice the small army gathered around working to help your child. And you will realize that what life gives you is people.

These people have entered from all directions and taken on a host of different roles. When Erin was a baby, before we knew of her disability, we had a sitter named Mary Lynn who was undeterred by Erin's failure to meet fine and gross milestones. Sensing my growing concern, Mary Lynn announced daily with unfounded confidence and a smile: "Next month she will walk!" Her enthusiasm kept me from dwelling and hopeful about Erin's development and not long after hopeful about my unborn son. I went on to have a happy and healthy second pregnancy and I credit Mary Lynn for that.

Early Intervention sent a consistent flow of young therapists eager to sort out Erin's sensory issues, strengthen muscle tone and motor skills, increase her ability to attend and focus and help her learn to communicate. After about a year of trial and error with different approaches and people, a small team formed and rallied around us. Nadine, Arlene, Jackie and Jill served as Erin's therapists but also my touchstones about everything related to Erin and eventually her brothers.

THE HELPERS

In those early days when new moms gathered for coffee and companionship, I relied on these women who arrived at our home with bags of books and games, strategies for work – and play and deep wells of encouragement and engagement for both of us. They cared for Erin intimately and were among the only people who could relate to how harrowing a haircut, holiday party or bus ride could be. With them I laughed and cried and learned how best to parent my daughter. Though I will never stop trying I can never thank them enough.

While most of Erin's army has been comprised of therapists, doctors, and other specialists, a rare few have been civilians, other moms. After several years of exclusive home-based therapy, as Erin's skills grew, her team agreed that play dates with peers from her mainstream preschool would be beneficial.

At first the thought of brokering this with other mothers was daunting. In New York City it's safe to say that kids and parents are looking to play up, not down. Erin was still mastering the art of turn taking and her self-regulation skills left a lot to be desired. An ideal or highly sought-after play mate she was not.

Erin was not the last kid to be picked, she wasn't even in the lineup. And as moms tend to be, I was protective of her – and her classmates. I was aware that a play date request could be challenging for kids who themselves were just learning to navigate the world outside their homes. Suggesting they do so alongside a kid who might start scattering toys or tantruming for no apparent reason seemed like an unfair ask.

I didn't float the idea past anyone until her second year at the nursery school – and then, so very gingerly – gauging reactions at school events or in passing on the street. If someone asked more than two questions about Erin, they were playdate potential.

As a mom of a special needs child, you're not looking for sympathy. That's the last thing you want, need or have time for. What you do want for your kid is a chance - someone willing to take a risk. All these years later I remain deeply appreciative of the moms who took the risk of having their kid 'play down' and hang out with a kid and mom who didn't have much to offer aside from juice boxes, snacks - and a bottomless well of thanks

The gratitude a parent feels for a person who takes the time to appreciate and help your child (typical or otherwise) truly knows no bounds. When we moved from the city we transitioned to a new team whose members we relied on to help Erin's language, motor and social skills continue to evolve. Highlights included speech with Roanne, OT with Debra, PT with Aresh and music with Angeline – who still brightens her schedule with songs today.

No week was complete without a trip to see our neighbors, Karen and Tom who welcomed Erin like one of their own children. They and their kids, Catherine, Tommy, Annie and Gracie greet her with bear hugs, share their books and stuffed animals, bake brownies, and play her favorite songs. Every visit Erin claps her hands in delight and life feels lighter. There are no advanced degrees or specialized training required to be a friend to a child with special needs – just a big heart and a person willing to open their door.

When Erin developed seizures at aged thirteen, however we did in fact require someone with a specialized degree. Two local nurses, Cliona and Julia, were assigned to take turns traveling to and from school with Erin each week. At a time when I was feeling most vulnerable, when my daughter had literally been seized by some unknown, unpredictable force, these angels arrived smiling on our doorstep every morning, happy to see Erin, ensuring me that whatever the ride might bring, they would be there for her, and me.

It is no easy journey – no parent expects it to be – but then there are the people who appear and offer you and your child their time, their understanding, their expertise, their patience, their optimism, and their love – and while it takes your breath away, it also builds you up. Gradually you feel that maybe you can handle it and, who knows, even take a stab at being that amazing mom – all thanks to them – the people that life or God gives you along the way.

"Before giving, the mind of the giver is happy; while giving, the mind of the giver is made peaceful; and having given the mind of the giver is uplifted."

Buddha

Happiness is a Bunch of Bananas

Erin furrows her brow as she sets groceries onto the checkout conveyer belt. Gently she places a container of raspberries mindful of the blueberries' unfortunate fall last week. When I motion to pick up a bunch of bananas, she pushes my hand away as if to say, *I got this mom.* I pull back and watch her empty the rest of the cart by herself.

At twenty-two there's still not much Erin does by herself, but like the rest of us she wants to do what she can and it makes her happy when she can help. "That was great!" she says as she heaves the last of the bags into the trunk of our car.

I thought of Erin and her shopping cart as I watched her brother and his classmates celebrate their recent high school graduation. In September he will enroll in college and study a wide range of subjects eventually honing in on a major, a discipline and a vocation. I hope whatever path he chooses to pursue he will feel the satisfaction, pride and happiness Erin experiences on a trip to *Stop 'n Shop*.

While Erin's brain works differently than the average high school or college graduate, how she derives happiness is the same. Aside from a steady stream of Disney movies and library visits, she wants nothing more than to apply the skills she's practiced for so long to everyday life, to contribute and to engage with those around her. This makes her happy.

Grocery shopping is one of the frequent and favored activities at her current day program. Together with her peers she delivers food and essentials to home bound seniors and a local soup kitchen. They also purchase ingredients for their weekly cooking class, which includes lessons in healthy food choices, setting a table, and practicing social skills.

As the past year has progressed I've seen her grow more interested and eager to engage in the life of our home. She wants to load and unload the dishwasher, to sort utensils, to put groceries away – often applauding herself with an "I did it!" or "That was awesome!" I understand that those headed for higher education might not get as jazzed by performing tasks like this, but these are the routines that keep a home humming along – and hopefully along with all the many achievements that lie ahead they too will similarly delight in making even the smallest contribution to a larger whole.

In recent years so much has been written and discussed about the nature of happiness and finding and living a fulfilling life. Whole college courses and careers are dedicated to the topic. One of the most compelling details of *The Blue Zone* study, an analysis of communities around the world where people live the longest and suffer lower rates of loneliness and depression, is the fact that community members cultivate a sense of purpose by sharing themselves and giving back to others - whether that be tending a communal garden, preparing a meal together or spending time with children, the elderly or infirm.

When it comes to my sons I often find myself saying, "I just want my kids to be happy." I've heard many parents say the same. Given today's sky-rocketing rates of anxiety and depression among teens and young adults it seems a reasonable wish.

Looking back on our past two decades with Erin though, I realize my concerns for her future have been less about her happiness and more about whether she would ever gain the skills necessary to form meaningful relationships and to make her own unique contribution to a family and community.

At aged two she cried through intensive ABA sessions as a therapist worked to pull her out of her own world and teach skills that came naturally to most. Sitting just steps outside the therapist's office in the cold lobby of an Upper West Side apartment building listening to her wail it took everything I had to keep from racing in, scooping her up and high tailing it out of there. It was torture for both of us, but over time she learned to make eye contact, to attend, to take turns and to follow two step directions – and to understand that there may be more to happiness than sitting at home surrounded by your toys.

Erin will always need support to get through her days and they are certainly not all sunshine and rainbows, but as we move into this next stage, not a day goes by that she doesn't try to do some small thing to connect, to contribute and to make someone smile.

Whether she's hoisting a bunch of bananas out of a grocery cart or asking the young man at the register: "What's your name?" Erin, along with a growing number of professors, publications and podcasts, reminds me what brings the greatest joy and meaning to our lives is not the ability to walk or talk on our own, but the desire and the ability to do so with – and for - others.

Author's Note

Ten years ago, I came across The Mighty, an online platform dedicated to people living with a wide array of life altering health conditions. In one of its early posts the journal asked readers: "If you could write a letter to yourself on diagnosis day what would you say?"

So, I dove in and wrote myself a letter about the day I learned my daughter was born with a rare condition that causes autism and a host of developmental delays. And then, a little bit like Forest Gump who just kept running, I just kept writing about life with Erin and her three younger brothers.

Parenting with or without a special needs child is not easy - and certainly never dull. I am grateful for publications like The Mighty for encouraging me and so many others to share our stories. Writing and reading about the small victories and inescapable disappointments of those traveling similar journeys is not only therapeutic, it's life affirming and joy inducing — and it certainly makes the whole endeavor feel a little less lonely.

Whether or not you're a parent of a special needs child, or a parent at all, I imagine our lives are more alike than they are different. The sun goes up, the sun goes down and in between we have a day. Whatever it may hold, there is beauty and wonder, friends and strangers to discover and to celebrate. I hope you've enjoyed and maybe see a bit of yourself and your loved ones in these stories - and wish you love, strength and grace along the way.

Acknowledgements

If it takes a village to raise a child, it's taken several to get where we are today. I am so grateful.

For teachers like *Maggie Donaghy* and the staff at St. Matt's BOCES for making Erin's last official school experience so full of love and happy days; *Allison Fish,* who brought exceptional passion and joy to her classroom and who conceived of the DEW Drop Deli allowing Erin to engage with the whole of Midland Elementary; *Nancy Godreau* for allowing Erin to 'play up' and go to school with her brother all those years ago.

For our ABA dream team: *Nadine Maher, Arlene Bradley, Jackie Arcarese* and *Jill Weynert* for their relentless efforts to pry the potential out of our girl, for understanding how hard a process it was for both of us - but never letting either of us off the hook; for *Roanne Zuckerman* and *Debra Beal* whose bright smiles and positive energy made our transition to the burbs and another in a series of pediatric therapy centers so seamless; for *Angeline Brown* who fills endless afternoons with the healing power of music; for Erin whisperer, *Orla O'Reilly* who saved us during quarantine and so many down days; for *Michelle Kjoller* who's led Erin on so many Cape Cod adventures; (and for fellow autism mom, *Antonia Bellanca*, for connecting us and for spotlighting the gold dust that is an afternoon at Fenway with the boys ... and *Eileen Heffernan* for leading me to Antonia and reminding me to walk on the bright side always.)

For doctors *Karen Kennedy, David Salsberg, Sue Hahm, Lauren Carton, Debbie Troy, Ronald Jacobson, Lee Cohen, Sandra Ang, Habib Jamal* and *Charles Soule* who've guided us through many dark and uncertain days with patience, kindness and expertise; for nurses (and friends) *Cliona Cronin* and the late *Julia Billingsley* whose love, commitment and sense of fun went far beyond any job requirement – and still do.

For our revolving door of caregivers who have stood in for the teachers, therapists, health care team – and me at all hours of the day, especially *Lerma Publico, Vangie Ochotorena, the "big" Erin Spadola, Mericel Elias, Tanya Morrison, Kristin Tobin,* and *Sandy Millman*. There are not enough words in any language to thank you for the care and kindness you have shown.

For creative thinkers and forces for good: *Jackie Ceonzo* of *SNACK, NYC* who saw that kids like Erin (and Joey) also need a place to play after school; *Amy Montimurro* of *ABILIS, Inc.*, where Erin continues to fill her days with purpose and joy; *Deb Rogan* and *Sofia Viola* of *Coffee for Good* which offers job training and work opportunities for young adults with disabilities; *Mike Porath* of

ACKNOWLEDGEMENTS

The Mighty for inviting so many in the special needs world to share their stories; and *Caroline Sandler* and *Maureen Mellett* at *Blue Path Service Dogs* for helping so many families like ours - and gifting us with our beloved *Pablo*.

For librarians everywhere especially those at the *Rye Free Reading Room*, the *Harrison Library*, the *Greenwich Library*, and the *Osterville Library* for their welcoming presence and unsurpassed patience in helping our very frequent flyer find all her favorite friends.

For other special needs parents, especially the members of the *Dup15q Alliance* and the *Land of Misfit Toys* who listen and share their experience with varying medications, behavioral approaches, schools and residential settings – and most of all for reminding each other we are not alone in our questions, struggles or the euphoria we feel in reaching any milestone - ever. Also, for friends especially at the boys' schools, who may not have special needs children but who get it, cut us some slack and cover for me time and again.

For our days, nights and friends at Windham Mountain, especially *Maura and Kevin Sheridan, Christine and Kevin O'Connor, Valerie and Scott McMurray* and the late, indomitable *Moreen Carey* who led us to the *Adaptive Sports Foundation* - where difference is not only welcome but celebrated

For writers like *Marek Fuchs* at Sarah Lawrence Writing Workshop who offered critical perspective outside the mom/friend/caregiver world; *Lee Woodruff* who took time to share her thoughts on life, parenting and these essays in the foreword - and encouraged me to take a breath and make this happen; *Robin Jovanovich* and *Jon Elsen* who enabled me to share so many stories about Erin with our community; and *Annabel Monaghan*: 'It is, indeed, an extraordinary thing to have a friend who is also a writer.' Thank you for sharing my love of words, (if not the Bardo), mulling them over and leading the way.

For our Rye 'treasure hunt' friends who helped keep Erin active and engaged when Covid took school and routine out of our lives, especially *"Jacquie"* whose mom, *Karen Quirke*, still brightens Erin's every Wednesday; line-editors, sounding boards and cheerleaders extraordinaire: *Lisi deBourbon, Caroline Findlay, Katie Fogarty, Val McMurray, Brooke Picotte* (who ran NYC for Erin and a lifetime of marathons with me), and our *91st St Gang*; for all our friends who have cheered Erin on all these years esp *Chris* and *Kathy McCormick* whose creativity and generosity in supporting Erin and her friends takes our breath away and *Karen* and *Tom Hamilton* who lived these stories with us, kept the lights on and opened their door and heart to Erin (and her mom) again and again - and who've never let the tie-dye well run dry.

For our extended *Flood-O'Connor Family* where Erin is and always has been just one of the pack – special thanks to Erin's crew

ACKNOWLEDGEMENTS

of mostly younger cousins who have graciously parted with favorite t-shirts, books, stuffed animals, *Disney* Princesses and so many *Sophie the Giraffes*; for my sister, *Carolyn Hoyos,* who never failed to show up for Erin here or across the pond; for Erin's (and my) biggest fan, my mom, *Maureen Flood,* who's been perfecting the art of behavior therapy for over fifty years and who, along with Pop-Pop, saved us countless nights with Erin, Will (and Pablo) sleepovers. (Life, and marriage, saver for sure.)

For best brothers, *Will, Patrick,* and *Jay,* for rolling with it when needed, throwing penalty flags when necessary and keeping us all moving full steam ahead. Finally, for crisis manager extraordinaire, my partner in all things Erin – and in all things - *Bill.* Thank you.

I am grateful to so many who have shared their stories, offering companionship and joy. Just to name a few...

Let Me Hear Your Voice, Catherine Maurice (Ballantine Books, 1994).

Thinking in Pictures: My Life with Autism, Temple Grandin (New York: Doubleday, 1995).

The Year of Magical Thinking, Joan Didion, (Vintage, 2007).

The Reason I Jump, The Inner Voice of a Thirteen-Year-Old Boy with Autism, Naoki Higashida (Random House, 2016).

Life Animated, Ron Suskind (Hyperion Avenue, 2016).

The Other Side of Impossible, Ordinary People Who Faced Daunting Medical Challenges and Refused to Give Up, Susannah Meadows (Random House, 2017).

Notes on Hope, Anne Lamott (Riverhead Books, 2018). (Or any book by Anne Lamott).

More Than You Can Handle, A Rare Disease, A Family in Crisis, and the Cutting-Edge Medicine That Cured the Incurable, Miguel Sancho (Penguin Random House, 2021).

Hard Landings, Looking into the Future for a Child with Autism, Cammie McGovern (Penguin Random House, 2021).

How to Be Human, An Autistic Man's Guide to Life, Jory Fleming (Simon & Schuster, 2021).

ACKNOWLEDGEMENTS

The Unlikely Village of Eden, Emma Nadler, (Central Recovery Press, 2023).

Stand by Me, A Guide to Navigating Modern, Meaningful, Caregiving, (Simon & Schuster, 2024).

The essays in this collection originally appeared in the following publications.

"A Letter to Myself on Diagnosis Day," *The Mighty*, 2016
"Eating Pizza Backwards" ("Why It's OK That My Sons Don't Always Love Their Sister's Autism,") *The Mighty*, 2015
"Groundhog Day," ("My Child has Autism. Here's How I Help Her Thrive,") *The Week*, 2016
"Look to the Strangers," ("To the Helpers Who Walk My Daughter Down the Hallway,") *The Mighty*, 2015
"A Pocket Full of Joy," ("My Daughter has Autism. At the library she found words and joy,") *The Week*, 2014
"A Dog Named Pablo, ("To the Family Member Who Helps Us Love – Not Fix – Autism,") *The Mighty*, 2014
"I am a Mom. I am that Mom. ("Mom Lets Child Escape into Gorilla Enclosure: I Am That Mom,") "*The Mighty*, 2016
"A Tale of Two Moms," ("Raising a Child with Autism,") *The Week*, 2014
"Road Trip," ("A Family Road Trip with My Daughter with Autism: A Journey of Love,") *Your Teen Magazine*, 2021
"Surviving a Special Needs Marriage, "*The Week*, 2016
Seizures and Silver Linings, ("Searching for the Silver Lining of My Daughter's Seizure Condition,") *The Mighty*, 2017

ACKNOWLEDGEMENTS

"Relying on Science, Going on Faith," ("We Live in a Space Between Questions and Answers for Our Medically Complex Children.") *The Mighty*, 2019

"Finding Awe in the Every Day," *The Rye Record*, 2023

"Finding Joy in Aisle Nine," *The Rye Record*, 2022

"Thirteen, ("When Your Special Needs Kid Becomes a Teen,") *The Week*, 2014

"Losing Pop-Pop," ("How My Teen with Autism Processes the Loss of Her Pop-Pop,") *Grown & Flown*, 2019

"A Time to Grow," *The Rye Record*, 2023

"Point to Happy," *The Rye Record*, 2022

"On Losing a Good Dog, "*The Rye Record*, 2022

"Lessons on Winning," *The Mighty*, 2021

"Magical Thinking," ("Years of Magical Thinking About Special Needs Daughter Are Over,") *Grown & Flown*, 2021

"Celebrating the Small Things this Christmas," ("What My Special Needs Daughter Taught Me About Christmas,") *The Week*, 2016

"Cookie Monster," *The Huff Post*, 2017

"The Helpers," ("To the Helpers Who Walk My Daughter Down the Hallway,") *The Mighty*,

About the Author, Eileen Flood O'Connor

Eileen grew up in Forest Hills, New York. She graduated from University of Virginia, holds an MA in English from the University of London and has worked as a writer at non-profits in Washington, D.C, and New York City. She lives in Westchester, New York with her husband, Bill, four children and Black Lab named Leo. Eileen writes about Erin, her family and other topics relevant to parenting – and life – today at eileenfloodoconnor.substack.com

About the Cover Artist, Patrick Ford O'Connor

Erin's younger brother, Patrick, attends college in Northern California where he studies Economics and Fine Arts, explores and photographs local beaches and hiking trails and coaches a Special Olympics Basketball Team. He continues to pursue his interest and passion for the arts and catalogues his work on Instagram at pocphoto_

www.ingramcontent.com/pod-product-compliance
Lightning Source LLC
LaVergne TN
LVHW041936070526
838199LV00051BA/2808